Getting through customs

Dedicated to
a great global family:
the International Fellowship
of Evangelical Students

Getting through customs

The global jottings of Chua Wee Hian

Inter-Varsity Press

INTER-VARSITY PRESS
38 De Montfort Street, Leicester LE1 7GP, England

First published 1992

British Library Cataloguing in Publication Data
A catalogue record for this book is available from the British Library.

ISBN 0-85110-869-5

Set in Linotron Baskerville

Photoset in Great Britain by Parker Typesetting Service, Leicester
Printed and bound in Great Britain by
BPCC Hazells Ltd
Member of BPCC Ltd

Inter-Varsity Press is the book-publishing division of the Universities and Colleges Christian Fellowship (formerly the Inter-Varsity Fellowship), a student movement linking Christian Unions in universities and colleges throughout the United Kingdom and the Republic of Ireland, and a member movement of the International Fellowship of Evangelical Students. For information about local and national activities write to UCCF, 38 De Montfort Street, Leicester LE1 7GP.

Contents

First shots

Personal snapshots

On a number of occasions, when passengers were asked to fill in their landing cards, under the section marked 'nationality' I have been tempted to write 'International' or 'Global'. Such entries might test the patience of the immigration officer.

I like to think of myself as a global Christian. For more than twenty-five years of international travel and ministry in different cultures, my horizons have widened and I have been gloriously enriched through personal contacts and friendships with Christians from different countries and cultures.

At heart, I am still thankful for my Chinese roots. I am also grateful for my adopted city and country – London, Britain – where I am now living. Some years ago on a radio interview I was asked when and where I first gained my international exposure. I thought hard and then mentioned 16 July 1939, the day I was born. The interviewer didn't expect that answer! When she had recovered her composure, she asked why I cited my date of birth as my entry into a fascinating international community. I explained that I was born in Singapore, which was then a British colony. The peculiar thing about Singapore is that it is a city, an island and now a republic all rolled into one. For over 150 years Singapore has been a cosmopolitan city, and, although racially I am Chinese, I grew up with Malay, Indian, Eurasian and European neighbours.

In my family I conversed in my provincial

13

Chinese dialect – Teochew – with my grand-mother and aunts. I spoke Cantonese to my mother and a mixture of Cantonese and Teochew to my father. When I was seven years old my parents were faced with a dilemma: should they send me to an English-stream or a Chinese-stream school for my education? In those days these linguistic streams flowed miles apart. My mother would have preferred me to go to a Chinese school where I would have been educated in Mandarin, but my father thought that in the long run my prospects would be much brighter if I studied English. It was only in high school that I had to study formal Chinese, but it was treated like a second language, and looking back it was rather curious that I had to study both Latin and Chinese.

The multi-ethnic community of Singapore meant that we had more religious and cultural holidays than most countries! My parents were very liberal in their views on education and their world view. That meant that my brothers, sister and I were encouraged to enjoy the greater world beyond Chinese society. We frequented restaurants which served international cuisine, and cultivated a gourmet taste for exotic food. Little then did I realize that this was part of my preparation for international bridge-building. As they say, the way to a man's heart is through his stomach. By enjoying local food one affirms the values of one's hosts' culture.

It was on Good Friday 1954 when it dawned on me that Christ died for our sins. Prior to that date, I had been a religious church-goer, confirmed in May 1953 and even assisting as a server at the Anglican Eucharist services. Looking back, I realize that it was through the reading of the

Scriptures that I entered into a personal relationship with the living Christ. Like most Christians in Singapore, my world view then was parochial.

My global horizons broadened when I was sent to London in 1957 to study business management. There I worked and studied alongside government scholars from the newly independent nations of Africa and Asia. I was fascinated by the wide range of accents when it came to communicating in the English language.

Later, when I decided to study theology, I found that in our college we had students from over fifteen countries. With a few others, I was involved in the formation of a new prayer group for international students. I served with the Inter-Varsity Fellowship team in befriending and welcoming overseas students, but I must confess that I was rather dissatisfied that they were operating primarily on the level of friendship. The fact that these students met only occasionally meant that they were not exposed to a systematic and consecutive presentation of the gospel.

So in 1959 I threw in my lot with the Chinese Church in London. At that time we were worshipping in the Central London YMCA and around twenty people would congregate in the chapel for a bilingual service. Through God's grace and providence a small committed core of students, together with Pastor Stephen Wang, were marvellously stirred by God. In 1960 over 100 Chinese students became Christians. At the Easter conference that year there was a sovereign visitation of the Holy Spirit. I remember it well because I was the chairman and, although the testimony service was scheduled for two hours, it turned into a six-hour event. I can never forget the scenes of people convicted by the Holy Spirit, confessing

15

their sins and repenting, and this was followed by a spirit of love amongst the members. 1960 was also an important year because the Chinese Church became an independent congregation, and we sought to direct its affairs along biblical lines. The extraordinary working of God's Spirit left a lasting impression on my life. God is truly alive and he longs to pour his Spirit on those who love him and seek to share his gospel with others.

In 1960 I worked together with some students from Singapore and Malaysia to start the Malaysian Christian Fellowship. Later, some of us also helped in the establishing of a sister fellowship – the Hong Kong Christian Fellowship. Again, unknown to me, God was using these pioneering experiences to prepare me for my later ministry, when I would have to encourage others in pioneering new student movements.

After graduating with a BD degree from the University of London, I was invited to serve as the associate pastor of the Chinese Church in London. For eighteen months the church saw steady growth. During this period I got engaged to King Ling. She was from Hong Kong and had become a Christian through her Christian Union at Bedford College in 1957. She was an exceptional student and completed her PhD degree in Chemistry when she was twenty-four. We were married on 15 September 1962, and a month later we returned to East Asia. We knew that God wanted us to return to minister to our own people.

From March 1963 I served as the only full-time staffworker of two young movements – the Fellowship of Evangelical Students of Singapore and FES-Malaya. For two and a half years King Ling and I were based in Singapore, where she was appointed Associate Professor at Nanyang University, a Chinese-speaking university. That gave us a unique opportunity to bring together the English-speaking and Chinese-speaking ministries in Singapore. At that same university we learnt how to spot and challenge promising students to serve the Lord Jesus Christ. Today, four of these students are heading up theological education in Singapore.

From Singapore we moved to Petaling Jaya, close to the University of Malaysia, where we ministered in the student world for twenty-one months. It was there that we made some deep and lasting friendships with many students and graduates.

On 1 March 1967 we moved as a family to Hong Kong. I was appointed first to work as special assistant to David Adeney, who was then the Associate General Secretary of IFES for East Asia. I succeeded him in August 1968. It was on the night that I was handed overall co-ordinating responsibilities for the region that our youngest son, Stephen, was born in Hong Kong.

East Asia was a huge parish and much time was spent travelling to encourage the growing movements. Some of the leaders, at first, were not used to a comparatively young leader. I was only twenty-eight then and I still remember older leaders in South Korea and Japan asking me my age.

During my brief stint as the East Asian Secretary I had the joy of encouraging the formation of two student movements in Thailand and Indonesia. With my base in Hong Kong, I naturally developed a deep interest in mainland China. I still have vivid recollections of going to a cinema in Hong Kong and watching a film about the cul-

17

tural revolution, seeing thousands and thousands of young people marching in the cities of China, holding banners and waving the red book *The Thoughts of Chairman Mao*, and almost deifying Chairman Mao. Their blind revolutionary zeal moved me to tears and I cried, asking God to turn the hearts of these young men and women to the true Lord – Jesus Christ.

In the summer of 1970, when I was invited to participate in an international students conference in Austria, C. Stacey Woods, who was then the General Secretary of IFES (International Fellowship of Evangelical Students), took me aside and told me that after much prayer and consultation, the Executive Committee would like me to become the next General Secretary. I stared at him incredulously. 'Me? You must be kidding! I'm just beginning to feel at home with my leadership responsibilities in East Asia.' Moreover, our family had just returned to Singapore to put down new roots. Surely IFES needed a more experienced person to lead it forward? But Stacey and other leaders assured me that I was God's man for this strategic responsibility. I told them that I needed time to talk and pray over this invitation with King Ling.

I was deeply touched when King Ling told me that she always wanted God's best for me, and that if he had called me to this job she would support me fully. I had reservations. As far as I knew, all successful international Christian organizations were led by people from either Europe or North America; could a young Singaporean Christian head up a growing international movement? It was with fear and trembling that I said 'Yes' to the Executive Committee. I was duly elected the second General Secretary of IFES in August 1971.

It was agreed that I should take six months off to study at the School of World Mission, Fuller Theological Seminary in Pasadena, California. Because of the flexibility of the American credits system, I was able to negotiate with my mentor Dr Arthur Glasser, who was also the new dean, to work for my MA degree in six months. Besides very heavy course work, I was also required to write a full-length dissertation. Those six months were enjoyable and valuable ones. I was introduced to fresh ideas about church growth, and the lectures and seminars on cultural anthropology provided me with invaluable tools as I sought to understand the different cultural situations in the IFES world.

Our family moved to London in August 1972 and for the next nineteen years I had the privilege of co-ordinating the growing work of IFES. In 1972 we had work in about sixty-five countries; today we have a viable witness in over 130 nations. A major emphasis of IFES ministry was to establish strong national movements so that there would be an ongoing student witness. In 1972 there were only forty member movements in the IFES family. Twenty years later there are ninety.

In my travels and meetings with student workers, students and graduates I gained new insights. I empathized with the struggles and problems which my colleagues faced. I observed the religious, cultural, social and economic obstacles which often impede the spread of the gospel. We were, of course, very excited when some of these were resolved with the enabling power of the Holy Spirit. Every visit was a new learning situation for me and over the years I grew to appreciate the rich and colourful tapestry of Christian service.

On my trips I am constantly dependent on my local hosts. These dear brothers and sisters have opened up new vistas for me. They have taken me not only into their homes but also into their hearts. I have gleaned precious information about family ties and kinship links and I am constantly intrigued by the intricate web of social relationships. So, inevitably, through my travels and interactions with people's customs I have tried to take global snapshots in my jottings. Some pictures are captured on my Ricoh SLR camera, but most are written in my private journals. Raw impressions have been repolished and framed for public viewing. When *Getting through customs* was being written, I had lunch with my editor, Colin Duriez, and also with the marketing manager, Paul Rusted. Both made very encouraging comments but they were flummoxed. They asked me, 'How shall we categorize and classify your book? Is it missions? Is it autobiography? Is it biography? Are these jottings reflections on leadership principles?'

I told them that it was a bit of each, but my desire is to share with you, the reader, the exuberance and wonder of serving God in his world, amongst his people. True, there are vignettes of joy and victory, but there are also tragic pictures of suffering. There are human and amusing 'snapshots'. You can also think through some of the more reflective passages which penetrate into the inner worlds.

Getting through customs in some ways is a team production. Without my colleagues and the local guides, this album of global 'snapshots' would never have seen the light of day. Equally, I am very grateful to those who have helped me in improving the presentation of the book. These include King Ling and our three sons – Andrew, Daniel and Stephen – and Mrs Alison Walley. A very special thanks goes to my secretary, Fiona Fisher, who in addition to 'organizing' a busy General Secretary, has willingly and patiently transcribed my dictated manuscript.

Chua Wee Hian

Harrow, Middlesex
February, 1992

1

Don't forget your L-plates

Portable ignorance

There was a time when I was very angry when I encountered Christian 'experts', who would go to a country to sell their packages. They are slick and glib; they give the impression that all the problems the local Christians face could be solved if only they would adopt their slogans or method of doing things. They are the gurus and have all the answers. Today, I don't get cross with them, but instead feel sorry for them. If they are honest they will confess to a spirit of staleness. Churning out the same stuff over and over again leads to boredom and stagnancy.

Whenever I travel or face new challenges, I often offer up this swift prayer, 'Lord, make me a learner. Don't let me take off my L-plates. I would like to glean new insights; teach me through the people I meet.'

I cherish Tom Wolfe, the distinguished American writer, who advised journalists to carry *portable ignorance* with them. Portable ignorance – what a marvellous phrase! That will stop me from appearing omnicompetent and feeling superior. When I assume the role of a learner, folks become more relaxed with me. They feel much freer to share with me their knowledge, experiences and insights.

The learner is a curious person. He doesn't just ask questions for information. He probes beneath externals, and he's keen to discover what makes a person or culture tick. He researches diligently and checks his sources before coming to a conclusion.

Some years ago at a press conference, a journalist asked the noted historian, Arnold Toynbee, 'Sir, what drove you to devote thirty-five years of your life to writing your great work – *A Study of History*?'

Toynbee rose from his seat and gave this penetrating reply: 'Curiosity.'

A little knowledge

In 1966, when I made my first ever visit to Bangkok, Thailand, a friend taught me some basic Thai phrases. Since I was keen to do some shopping I asked her to help me master the pronunciation of Thai numbers.

As it turned out, I discovered that most of the shopkeepers in Thailand were Chinese from my ancestral province, so I could buy and bargain for my jewellery and souvenirs in my own dialect. But all the pedicab drivers were indigenous Thai and therefore could not speak Chinese. I was rather amused when my American lecturer friend asked me to bargain for a pedicab. She stood several metres away from me. She spoke fluent Thai, but knew that all the pedicab drivers would charge us a much higher fare if she negotiated it. So I glowed with pride as I successfully bargained with the pedi-cab driver to take us back to where I was staying for a very reasonable price.

The following day I was on my own, shopping, and I wanted to try out my skills in negotiating a ride back to my hotel. Everything went smoothly; the driver knew where to take me, and we had both agreed to the fare. As we approached the hotel, I suddenly realized that I had not learnt the Thai word for 'Stop'. The driver was stepping on his accelerator. I yelled 'Stop' in Chinese, hoping that it might sound Thai. He rode on and I had to use my arms frantically to signal to him to stop. He had to apply the brakes abruptly; we had overshot my hotel by several metres. As I got out of his carriage a torrent of Thai words flowed from his lips. I couldn't understand what he said, but I guess he was ticking me off for not giving him earlier notice to stop. I waved a polite goodbye and an apologetic thank you as I walked sheepishly back to my hotel.

A terrifying curse

I read somewhere (it's strange how odd bits of information stick in one's mind, but the source is forgotten) of a rather frightening curse uttered by the Tartar tribe in the steppes of Central Asia: 'May you stay in one place for ever.'

It is indeed a curse to allow ourselves to be hem-med in, impervious to new ideas and rejecting the challenge of new horizons. It's like calcifying in a fixed mould.

Isn't it sad that in many churches today we apply the age-old liturgical phrase to the way we see and do things: 'As it was in the beginning, is now and ever shall be . . .'

2

As others see us

God of flowers

Hanna Lee became a Christian whilst studying in London. When she returned to Hong Kong she was keen to wean her mother off her idolatrous habits.

'Mamma, why do you offer roast pork and bottles of cognac and brandy to these Chinese deities? You and I know that they cannot eat and drink your offerings.'

Her mother replied, 'My dear daughter, these sacrifices are simply symbolic. We enjoy eating roast pork. Your father entertains his business clients with Napoleon brandy. Who knows? Perhaps the spirits will be pleased with our gifts and will reward us because of our piety.'

One day Hanna decided to take her mother to a local church. She was confident that the latter would be impressed by the beauty and simplicity of the church set-up. Later, at lunch, Hanna was eager to find out about her mother's first impressions of church life.

'Yes, I liked the music; the people were quite

friendly. But I must say that I am rather curious about your Christian customs. I think your God is very Western. Unlike our Chinese gods, who prefer roast pork, brandy and cognac, yours seems content with the scent of flowers. What a paltry offering — two baskets of flowers offered by two hundred people to their God!'

A strange proposal

My colleague, E., was in Trinidad, and part of her brief was to teach and encourage Christian students to share the good news of Jesus. One afternoon they decided to do some practical fieldwork that would give all the participants an opportunity to share their faith. In Trinidad, because most folks are warm and friendly, there was no problem in striking up conversations with people on the streets. E. began talking to a young Trinidadian and asked him if he knew God personally. He admitted that he had lost his spiritual bearings. But he immediately added that he was eager to return to God. E. explained the way of salvation to him, whereupon he unexpectedly popped the question, 'Will you marry me? I could do with a missionary wife who will help me along life's way.'

If Adam and Eve were Chinese

Chinese Christians are often puzzled by Peter's reaction to his peculiar vision of a large sheet with strange birds, animals and reptiles in it (see Acts 10:9–14). Worse was to come, because in his vision he heard a voice commanding him to kill and eat these creatures. Because of his strict Jewish upbringing and his scruples, the very thought of eating 'unclean' meat struck fear into his heart. I once heard a Chinese preacher explain that for him and many others eating that odd collection of birds, animals and reptiles would be a gourmet's delight! He went on to make this astute observation: 'If Adam and Eve had been Chinese, there would have been no fall and therefore no sin in the world.'

When asked the reason for his statement, he calmly replied, 'They would have eaten the snake!'

Your church is too dull

I wonder how local churches would react if they were asked to conduct a market research survey in their area. Christians have heard the familiar groans and quips as to why people do not go to church. Two pastor friends decided to find out and so they sent sensitive members to ask unchurched people why they did not go to church. The majority of the respondents cited the following reasons:

- The services are too dull.
- The message is often irrelevant.
- The church is always asking for money.
- Everything is so predictable.
- The worshippers are so cold.
- We don't really feel welcomed.

Some Christian leaders would write off such surveys and reinterpret the unchurched rejection in theological terms: 'The god of this world has blinded their hearts and minds.'

'They are so steeped in worldly matters that they have no time for God.'

'They are not "the elect"!'

Are we justified in using these theological analyses to back up our *status quo*? If our churches are not sharing the good news of Jesus in an attractive and meaningful way, should we not have a second look? Why is it that some churches that have taken their market survey seriously and introduced lively worship, contemporary music and drama, preaching that touches real-life human problems, and who are prepared to adapt their services to attract the unchurched, see new folk coming in to their services?

All preachers great and small

The dome-shaped gym at the University of Illinois, Urbana, was crammed with over 18,000 people. All eyes were on me as I gave a ten-minute report of what God was doing in the world of students. The noble team of technicians dutifully beamed me across five or six huge screens. My image was literally blown up.

Later, when the meeting was over, a crowd of students milled around the speakers. Some were asking questions while others were seeking autographs. A student approached me, and when she saw my 'Speaker' label she queried, 'Were you the guy who spoke to us a few moments ago about student work?'

I nodded and simply said, 'Yes, that was me.'

'Now that I see you, you look so ordinary.'

It was a realistic, down-to-earth comment. And it was also good for my humility.

It was like a bazaar

After months of friendship, I took a Muslim student to a lively evangelical church in London. The evening service was a special guest service at which the gospel would be faithfully proclaimed. Both of us were rather nervous and apprehensive as we entered the packed church. The service itself was impressive and the message was clear, concise and convincing. Afterwards, as we went to a café for coffee, I asked my friend what he thought of the service. He hesitated and I asked him to be brutally frank with me. I shall never forget his reply. 'It was the first time I've been to church. I was struck by the large number of young people who were there, but my spirit was troubled and vexed. No, it was not because of our different creeds, but because of the atmosphere. Unlike the mosque, where we carefully prepare ourselves to worship Allah, the great and mighty God, I felt as if I was in a bazaar or market. People were chattering away. It was so difficult to try and worship God amid such a din.'

My, you really know God!

On another occasion I brought two Irish students to the local church where I was worshipping regularly. After the sermon we were asked to break up into small groups for prayer and sharing. I muttered a few words to these two friends, hoping that they would not be embarrassed by spontaneous, extempore prayers. After a brief period of sharing, the four church members in that small group prayed. Afterwards, when the Irish students were asked for their impressions, they remarked, 'We were startled to find ordinary Christians enjoying such intimate contact with God. You certainly seem to know him. We wish we could talk to him the way you do.'

In subsequent months one of them did become a committed Christian, but it was interesting that it was the experience of Christians opening their hearts and lifting their voices to God that drew him to a deep relationship with the living God.

3

All things to all men

That's too sexy!

Doug and Marilyn Stewart have been working among students in Mexico City since 1971. One day they decided to go to a growing Pentecostal church near their home. It was packed with people and the worship was joyful and enthusiastic. After the breathless rounds of singing, clapping and foot-stomping they were glad to be able to sit down.

In his normal, relaxed way, Doug crossed his legs and listened intently to someone giving her testimony. Suddenly, a steward came along with a short pole in his hand. Without any warning, he prodded Doug's upper left thigh so that the entire leg rested on the ground again. At first Doug thought that the steward was simply being playful, so he recrossed his leg. Within seconds the same steward uncrossed Doug's leg, and this time my co-worker was most upset.

'What's the matter?' he asked.

The reply was curt and sombre. 'You were sitting with your legs crossed and that's a very sexy pose.

It's indecent to sit that way in the house of God.'

Doug blushed and, before he could reply, a lady usher rushed up and threw a blanket around Marilyn's shoulders. She protested, 'I'm not cold. In fact, it's quite warm in here.'

The usher gave her a matronly stare and rebuked her, 'Don't you know it's indecent to come to church in a blouse with short sleeves? Next time please wear a long-sleeved one.'

There was no next time . . .

Skirt and hair lengths matter

In September 1968, soon after assuming responsibilities as Associate General Secretary of IFES for East Asia, I received a letter from my chief, C. Stacey Woods. He had received a report from a missionary participant at our East Asian conference. This participant was horrified that lady participants, including IFES lady staff, could wear skirts above the knee. This complaint was registered in the late sixties when mini-skirts were the height of fashion.

My colleague, Ada Lum, was going to central Asia the following year. I shared Stacey's letter with her. Our emotions were similar – a mixture of laughter, anger and concern. So I said to Ada, 'Sister, you're going to have a problem next year. What clothes are you going to take to India?'

She calmly replied, 'I don't think that I can cope with long-length saris; washing would be a problem, but I'll go to my tailor's right away.' She ordered two or three maxi-skirts. To turn up in India with shorter hem-line dresses would prove offensive and disrupt fellowship.

By contrast, a group of young Christian musicians

33

were booked for a series of evangelistic concerts in Singapore. The authorities had decreed that men with long hair should not be allowed to perform or speak at public functions. When this troupe landed at the airport, they were told by the immigration officers that they could only perform if they had their hair trimmed, since their hair was longer than the specified length. They were most upset and felt that the Singapore government had contravened personal and social rights. As a protest, they flew on to their next destination leaving the local Christian organization to handle the crisis of a broken engagement.

Ladies, no trousers!

Lady staff have found how useful jeans or slacks are when working in countries infested by mosquitoes. Bare flesh can be a gourmet feast for these insects! But we have to advise our international travellers not to wear jeans or slacks when they visit parts of Nigeria. Here many church leaders and Christian young people take the Mosaic injunction in Deuteronomy 22:5 literally: 'A woman must not wear men's clothing, nor a man wear women's clothing, for the LORD your God detests anyone who does this.'

Wrong spirit

Alcoholic drinks can stir up bitter controversy. Once when I was present at an international conference in Austria, the leadership team sought my advice. African Christians were horrified that the conference centre sold beer and served wine to certain guests. They thought it was most unchristian to serve the demon spirit of alcohol and wanted the leaders to ban it. They declared dogmatically that it was the wrong spirit for an international Christian conference.

At the same conference our team received written suggestions from the Spanish delegation; they were very disappointed because table wine was not served with the midday and evening meals. They urged that the situation be rectified as soon as possible.

It would have been tempting to study the Scriptures on wine. There are verses which describe wine as making glad the heart of man (Psalm 104:15). Jesus' first miracle was to turn six huge jars of water into wine (John 2; according to the NIV footnote at verse 6, between 450 to 690 litres of vintage wine). Paul urged Timothy to take some wine for his stomach (1 Timothy 5:23). I'm always fascinated by anti-wine Christians, insisting that this wine was no more than unfermented grape juice. In the case of Timothy, one resourceful commentator remarked that the wine was 'not for internal consumption but for external application'.

Equally, the Scriptures do warn against drunkenness and excessive imbibing of strong drinks (see Isaiah 5:11, 22 and Ephesians 5:18) and causing our brothers to stumble by what we eat or drink (Romans 14:20, 21).

In the end I suggested that African Christians and the Spanish folk should have an informal Bible study on Romans 14. That proved to be a wonderful solution to their debate.

4

Roots and shoots

Good shoots

To be global Christians, we need to rejoice in our
roots. In one sense, we did not choose to be born
English, American, Indian, Chinese or whatever.
But we all have family roots.

During the early seventies a very fine American
missionary applied to join our fellowship. He was
well-trained and in many ways remarkably sensitive
to the values of other cultures. However, I felt
rather uncomfortable when he began to denigrate
his American roots. His country was then engaged
in a protracted war in Vietnam. The image of the
ugly American was universally transmitted. He was
ashamed of his country's foreign policies; he publicly confessed that he wished he weren't an American citizen.

In July 1974 this same man attended the
Lausanne Congress on World Evangelization. From
the platform American brands and 'packages' of
Christianity were critically exposed and fiercely
attacked by leaders from Latin America and Africa.

Some of the criticisms, I realize, were below the belt. The missionary was deeply hurt and his entire perspective changed. From then on he adopted an implacable right-wing, flag-waving patriotic American position. Soon he began to sever his links with Christian leaders from the Two-Thirds World. He is now pastoring a church in the USA and, as far as I know, he is low-key on missions.

That violent swing in his identity pendulum was a grim reminder to me to be aware of those who cannot appreciate both the strengths and weaknesses of their racial and cultural roots. As Christians we must be able to thank God for the good things in our heritage.

Bad shoots

Ethnocentrism is defined by Louis Luzbetak as 'excessive group-centredness – the natural tendency in man to evaluate one's own in-group and its behaviour and interests as superior to those of other groups.' This feeling of superiority is generally subconscious, but only too often expressed in a word or action: 'Our form of government is the best in the world.'

'Our educational system makes the local universities look like kindergartens.'

'Our cooking cannot be equalled.'

Dr Luzbetak goes on to expose this dangerous shoot:

> Group-centredness becomes particularly dangerous when it drives a group, as it only too often does, to re-educate the out-group 'to make everyone as great as myself!' What an ideal! British want to anglicise all

non-Britishers; the Germans want to ger-
manise every non-German; the Americans
feel it is their God-given mission to ameri-
canise every non-American. Everyone
wants to re-educate everybody else according to his own image and likeness.[1]

I find myself constantly having to battle against
my in-group superiority or ethnocentrism when a
meeting is badly organized or when budgets are not
met. I would compare them unfavourably with my
inherited skills as an organizer. When a fellowship
struggles with its finances and does not appear
resourceful in managing its affairs, I would sub-
consciously glory in Chinese competence in generating finances and marshalling strong
organizational support. On a number of occasions
my entrepreneurial abilities saved the day, but in
my perversity I forgot that it was God who gave me
those skills and opportunities in the first place. So I
resolutely refuse to compare the strong points of my
culture and social background with the weak points
of other cultures. I find myself enthusiastically
identifying with Dr Luzbetak when he writes:

I will at all times try to see the beauty in the
Creator's human kaleidoscope. I will at all
times try to appreciate the variety of flowers
in God's human garden; they are all attractive, even if they are not all roses like myself.
If God is delighted with differences in
human beings, I must be too. I will at all
times, therefore, try to see the divine
humour in allowing mankind to be so varied
– so different from me.[2]

38

Local ginger is never hot

At our World Assembly in 1987, several African delegates pressed us to issue certificates for those who had attended our international staff training conferences. I almost stood up to challenge this request. Some of us are only too familiar with postal institutions that set up bogus colleges issuing fake diplomas or even degrees, provided a suitable fee is paid. My instant reaction was negative. But I bit my tongue, restrained my body and listened to the proposals. It soon transpired that church leaders in their countries do not believe that 'any good can come out of Nazareth', that is, from their local setting. A high premium is awarded to anyone who has been trained overseas, especially in England. Again I registered a mental protest, 'Uh-oh, that smacks of the colonial past.'

Afterwards I had further opportunities to discuss with my African brothers and also delegates from other continents. They adamantly reinforced the Chinese saying, 'Local ginger is never hot'. Or, in biblical language: 'No prophet is acceptable in his own country' (Luke 4:24, RSV).

In 1989, when we held our staff training conference in London, we issued diplomas to all who had attended our courses and worked through the assignments. These certificates are now neatly framed and adorning the walls of several homes. Amazingly, both students and church leaders look to the owners of these certificates with greater respect because they have received training in London.

5

On being Chinese

Foreign devils

The eminent psychoanalyst, Carl Jung, often lectured and wrote on the influence of race-consciousness in every person. For me, to belong to a race with a long history and great size (one out of every five people in the world is Chinese) is often mind-boggling! Sometimes, when I step out of my psyche and look at myself as objectively as possible, I muse, 'Do I share some of the dominant characteristics of the Chinese people?'

For centuries, China, the world's largest nation, has described itself as the Middle Kingdom. My ancestors firmly believed that other nations which inhabited territories outside this great land were benighted, uncultured and unlearned. So racial superiority is inbred in every Chinese.

Living in Singapore, where 80% of the population are Chinese, this spirit was drummed into my system. Whenever I spoke to my Chinese friends we referred to all other races as 'devils'. But when I developed a Christian mindset, I found this description of other races and people terribly repugnant. There are drawbacks too when it comes to communication with one's own people. I recall travelling to a village in neighbouring Malaysia where I was keen to locate two English missionaries. I stopped at a market and approached a fruit-seller, and asked her whether she knew where two English missionaries were staying. She shook her head, but a customer overheard me and asked me to repeat my question. I did so. She paused for a few moments and then her face lit up and she exclaimed, 'You mean those red-haired foreign devils?' I gave an embarrassed nod and soon they were directing me to the missionaries' home.

Back to the motherland

It was in July 1982 that I made my first visit to mainland China. When we were living in Hong Kong in the late sixties I had always looked across the border and longed for the day when I could return to the motherland. That wish was probably echoed by millions of overseas Chinese. In the earlier part of our century many of my forefathers had left southern China to work in South-East Asia. After they had made their fortune the men, who by then had become patriarchs of their families and clans, would return to their ancestral village in China. They would spend their remaining few years there and their deep desire was to be buried on home soil.

I wasn't thinking of my future burial spot, but I was keen to see something of the culture and history of my people. Accompanied by King Ling and our two younger boys, we made our six-day pilgrimage to Beijing. We were on a conducted tour. As tourists, our guides escorted us and their task was to show us China, ancient and modern. As we stood in the famous Tian-an-men Square my mind was filled with images of the cultural revolution, when thousands upon thousands of soldiers and young people had waved their red books and chanted their adulations to Chairman Mao. He had almost become a living deity. His words were 'infallible'.

I remember being led to the huge marble hall where the body of the late Chairman Mao was housed in a glass chamber. Tourists and Chinese citizens filed slowly and silently by, gazing at this man. I was astonished at how small he was, because before entering the hall I had seen a huge sculpture of him towering over the long queues of sightseers. This was the man whose voice and words had shaken the nation, and whose power gave pride and self-respect to the Chinese people in establishing the People's Republic. He had erased over a century of humiliation and subjugation of the Chinese people by both the Japanese and the West. As a Christian I disagreed, of course, with the way in which he had ruled so harshly, and I was critical of his poor leadership, especially towards the end of his life. But the guide reminded us that it was Mao who had made the Chinese people great again.

I was happy to subscribe to this theme of greatness when I walked in pelting rain across several hundred metres of the Great Wall. I remembered that the American astronauts reported that this was the only man-made structure that was visible when they orbited around the earth. Its architecture and durability produce a sense of pride in this colossal achievement.

From our tour of the Great Wall we were taken to see a few of the famous Ming tombs. These had been excavated only a few decades before and we were privileged to see what was inside one. Each tomb was almost like a miniature aerodrome and we were told that thousands of workers were employed to build them. We had to pinch ourselves when we saw the treasures that were on display. The gold jewellery with precious stones gleamed and glowed. We saw boulders (yes, huge rocks) of precious jade. For the Chinese this is probably the most precious of stones, and jade rings, amulets, bangles and neck-laces were very often buried alongside their owners. So there I was, working out how much 100kg of pure jade would cost in the open markets of Hong Kong. And as I looked at the jewellery, I admired the craftsmanship and skills of jewellers in the 12th and 13th century AD.

But suddenly my admiration turned to a deep sense of revulsion. The guide told us that after the tomb had been completed all the workers were taken to another site. They were asked to dig a huge hole and all of them were either killed or buried alive in this pit. It took me quite a while to recover from this chilling tale.

My spirit rose from revulsion to exultation and wonder when we looked at the Heavenly Temple where emperors would commune with heaven's deities. Obviously, it was not their piety or religion which I admired, but the structure itself. As I stretched my neck and peered at the immense height, and as I scanned its intricate patterns and the architecture of this tall building which had stood the ravages of time and the elements, our tour party was told that the entire edifice was built without a nail or a screw joining two pieces of wood together.

Now, when we joined that tour, we did so as overseas Chinese. That meant that we were given

Chinese cuisine and our guides would speak Cantonese (since we'd booked our tour in Hong Kong this was the lingua franca). But all through the tour we were made to feel very welcome. We were more than honoured guests; we were told that we belonged to our motherland.

But why didn't the overseas Chinese stay? The reason was obvious. We saw the other side of China. Beijing's citizens exude a monotone ordinariness. In 1982 a lot of people were still wearing drab blue trousers and shirts, including the women. Hundreds of people were fighting for seats on buses and on the underground trains. If we had tried to find our way to the tourist spots as ordinary citizens of China we would have had to queue for hours, whereas as tourists we were given VIP treatment all the way.

Mistaken identity

In my international travels I am fascinated by the deference and politeness which many immigration officers and shopkeepers show me. At first I thought that the local people were simply very friendly and courteous, but when my host told me that they were normally rude to folk from their own countries or continents, I began to ask questions. In each case the answer has been the same – I have been mistaken for a Japanese.

Bless them, the Japanese are great tourists. They are also known to be generous spenders and cause very few problems wherever they go. Their companies reward them for loyal service, and they travel, normally in groups, to different parts of the world. Once when I was in Christchurch, New Zealand, I inquired about the price of pure woollen sweaters. I was taken aback when the price quoted was about three times higher than I would pay in London. Since I was the only tourist, I asked the lady owner, 'Tell me, do you sell many of these, especially at these prices?' She nodded and assured me that my compatriots from Japan would normally buy two apiece. Perhaps she thought that I was rather un-Japanese, or even rather stingy!

Here in London I am surprised that most Chinese who are looking for lodgings find it extremely easy to rent rooms or apartments. Again, we have all been mistaken for Japanese.

Now, I know that some of you might be asking, 'How does one distinguish between a Japanese and a Chinese?' It's not easy, but my Japanese colleague, Koichi Ohtawa, volunteered this answer when asked by an Australian: 'The Chinese tourist has one camera and the Japanese tourist has two.'

In 1969 I visited Koichi Ohtawa and his team of student workers in Tokyo. I was about to catch the bullet express from Tokyo to Osaka when a Japanese lady, clad in a kimono, ran up to me and frantically asked me about where she could catch a train, the correct platform, *etc.* She was surprised when I shrugged my shoulders and shook my head. She almost fainted when my co-worker and good friend, David Michel from New Zealand, immediately stepped in and gave her a satisfactory reply, in Japanese, to her questions. The poor lady looked even more confused, so I nudged David and urged him to explain that I was not Japanese but Chinese. When David offered this explanation she sighed with relief.

Inscrutability

If I were to ask my non-Chinese friends what they thought of the Chinese, most of them would probably reply with one word, 'Inscrutable'. Our Confucian upbringing has taught us to suppress our feelings. Since face and respect are very important, a Chinese, in whose blood is instilled all the teaching and customs of Confucian ethics, would find it very difficult to say 'No' to a request. So if a zealous Western Christian were to invite a Chinese friend to a special Christian meeting, the latter would probably say 'Yes' and not show up. Why then did he reply in the affirmative? The simple answer is that he did not want his Western friend to lose face and for their friendship to be spoilt. So the most difficult instructions that I have to share and communicate with my fellow Chinese Christians are to let our 'Yes' be yes and our 'No' be no.

Inscrutability has some advantages. When I first visited Africa and Latin America most of the Christians there did not know how to respond or relate to me initially. They were curious because most of the mission executives who visited them were Westerners. The local Christians knew how to size them up and patronize them: if they hold important positions, they must be loaded with bags of gold and US dollars.

I shall never forget speaking at the Christian Union meeting in Dar es Salaam, Tanzania. I shared my testimony and expounded Scripture. Afterwards, a student got up and almost trumpeted before the whole audience these startling words, 'Brother Chua, you are most welcome to our country. We see you smiling when you speak. There is so much of the Lord's joy in you.' I must admit that I blushed a little.

Afterwards I asked this student what she had meant. She explained, 'Here in our country we see hundreds of Chinese workers building the railway line from the coast to Zambia. These Chinese workers are unapproachable. They are aloof and, I think, look down on us. They never smile and we think that they are like aliens from outer space. When I saw you and heard you speaking I almost wanted to jump up and walk down to you, and to touch you to see whether you were real. I have never met a Chinese Christian before.'

Exported goods

The only visit that I ever paid to Haiti was in March 1976. Not being able to speak French or the native Creole, I was rather restricted. My host was a busy lecturer and was out for most of the day. Normally I love to wander round my new environment, especially to meet the local people, so at mid-morning I decided to leave the safety of my hotel and to wander into the nearby town. I had hardly walked more than twenty steps when I was sur-rounded by twenty young Haitian boys. I wasn't afraid or overwhelmed by young boys running to greet or talk to me. What scared the life out of me was when all these twenty boys suddenly adopted Chinese martial art poses and formed a ring around me. For a while my heart was in my mouth and I had to pray for wisdom. Then, suddenly, a few of them shouted, 'Kung-fu! Kung-fu!' and the others echoed, 'Bruce Lee! Bruce Lee!' I burst into laughter. I quickly pointed to myself and using sign language made it clear that I was no Bruce Lee and no expert in martial arts.

Later in the day, when my host took me around

Port au Prince, I saw the cinema hoardings advertise Chinese films featuring Bruce Lee, Jackie Chen and the Shao Lin warriors. I felt rather sad that all the Chinese people could export to this poor nation were kung-fu films.

I must say, however, how glad I was when I was sight-seeing and shopping along the borders of Togo and Ghana in August 1988. I was the victim, like many others, of mosquito bites and my arms were full of little lumps. I had my regular malarial pills so I wasn't afraid of catching this dreaded disease, but I was longing for a balm that could soothe the irritations from the mosquito bites. I thought to myself that if I was in Singapore I would have used the famous tiger balm. I made a mental note that I should keep a round box of this ointment with me. Now most Chinese believe that this particular balm can cure headaches, toothache, rheumatism and also insect bites. Imagine my surprise when I saw that a local stall-holder was selling tiger balm made in Singapore. I bought a box and began to apply it to my skin. I couldn't help extolling its virtues and potency to my African friends!

Reading the Bible – the Chinese way

At services and meetings where I try to encourage people to read and obey God's Word, I say to them, 'The best way of reading the Bible is the Chinese way.' A dramatic pause follows. Then I point out that most people will read their Bibles looking at the text from left to right, and if they are Jewish or Arab from right to left. But in the case of Chinese Christians, because our text is written from top to bottom, we read the Bible in the correct way. Every time we we read the Bible in the correct way. Every time we read God's Word we are nodding our heads, we are saying 'Yes' to God's promises, 'Yes' to his warnings, 'Yes' to his commands and promptings.

What's in a name?

It was in late 1989 that I learnt to my dismay that I had a name which is too foreign and unpronounce-able to be remembered by people other than those who live in Singapore and Malaysia. Names like John Stott and Billy Graham are much easier to recall and quote.

I shall never forget Hans, a German student, who was asked to chair an evening meeting at an inter-national conference in Austria. His zeal for accuracy and thoroughness amazed me. Hans spent half an afternoon trying to memorize my full name; he pronounced it over and over again.

Then came the evening session. As he got up to introduce me, in English, suddenly his demeanour changed. He was seized by stage fright and I could almost see the invisible tentacles of language stran-gling his composure. He only managed to verbalize my family name 'Chua' and then found himself tongue-tied. He felt embarrassed and tried again. It was semi-intelligible. He went on to describe some of my responsibilities and experiences as an inter-national speaker and traveller. His final line was, 'Now I'm going to hand this part of the meeting to Mr Chua . . . (a long pause) . . . Chua Whatever-his-name-is.' It wasn't a total disaster, because there was mirth and sympathetic laughter.

I didn't have the heart to tell Hans about Mala-gasy names. Solomon Andria is IFES Regional Secretary for Francophone Africa. I'm thankful he's shortened his family name to Andria as it's simple to remember, but his friends and relatives address him as 'Solomon Andriatsimialoman-anarivo'. It's not uncommon to have family names averaging twenty-four letters!

I suppose in cross-cultural situations some names can cause untold mirth. Another German friend, Professor Bodo Volkmann of Stuttgart, a former chairman of the IFES Executive Committee, was once invited to give lectures in mathematics at the University of Malaysia. He was sponsored by the Goethe Institute. Being a man who enjoys a joke, I warned him that his name would cause ripples of laughter amongst Malaysian students. 'Bodo' in Malay or Indonesian means stupid, or fool. True to his humour, Professor Volkmann exploited his own Christian name, Bodo, to great advantage. When I visited him in his home in Stuttgart some years later, he proudly showed me a press clipping with the title, 'This professor is no Bodo.'

On my first visit to Vietnam, the Vietnamese Christian students were singing lustily and I heard 'chua' being sung. As I looked at the romanized script there were numerous references to 'chua' in the hymn. I flipped through the hymnbook and again 'chua' caught my eye. I raised this with the staffworker after the meeting, asking him the meaning of the word. I was delighted when he told me it meant 'the Lord'.

On the other hand, 'chua' has a very different meaning in Hindi. I observed that my Indian friends called me Mr Wee Hian instead of Mr Chua. Our eldest son, Andrew, who worked in an international bank in Calcutta and Bombay, also told me that he was called Mr Andrew by his colleagues at work. They avoided calling him Chua because in Hindi it means 'rat'.

I have also discovered that titles are very important to certain people. In Japan you need to show great respect to older people, addressing them as '*sin seh*'. One rarely uses first names. I have had Chinese and Korean pastors who got rather upset with me because I didn't address them as Pastor so-and-so or the Reverend so-and-so. So when I am in a new culture I seek to find out how I should be addressing the most senior people.

But I have been surprised to receive letters from some African staff who address me as Big Brother Chua Wee Hian. There is no Orwellian undertone in such a title! It is, in fact, a term of respect and endearment. It must be difficult for those in the West to appreciate the importance of using names correctly with their corresponding titles. I shall never forget the horrified look of a Chinese professor from Taiwan when he heard my son's fellow students at Oxford calling their tutors by their Christian names. Later, when we were in a restaurant, he queried, 'Aren't the English students taught good manners at home or at school? How could they address their teachers by their first names?'

Names in many cultures spell identity and titles, social status. Remembering names and addressing peers and seniors correctly bolsters relationships.

'Wiseman Wee?'

Soon after my appointment as General Secretary of IFES, I was introduced to Bob (not his real name), an American Christian public relations consultant. My friend who introduced us assured me that he had an admirable track record. Bob had helped several Christian organizations to increase their income. He might be just the man to jack up the much needed finances for our Fellowship.

Over lunch Bob exuded confidence and sweetness. He was impressed by the goals and vision of our worldwide student ministry. There was a lot going for IFES, but there was one major problem. American Christians often associate the president or chief executive officer with the organization itself. He gravely commented, 'With a long name – The International Fellowship of Evangelical Students – and a foreign name like Chua Wee Hian, you have two strokes against you.'

Bob was convinced that there was little difficulty for prospective donors to get used to IFES. He went on, 'But how do we sell Chua Wee Hian?' I shrugged my shoulders. Suddenly he became rather excited, 'Isn't it true that Chinese names have special meanings attached to them?' I nodded and explained that my given names 'Wee Hian' meant 'Great Sage'.

'Terrific!' he exclaimed. 'Now the Christian world is familiar with Watchman Nee. He's admired, and his books are widely available. If you were to change your name to "Wiseman Wee", we could make you a celebrity!' I firmly declined his ingenious attempt.

6

The land of the rising sun

Ancient and modern

Japan exudes a mysterious and mystic aura for me. I have visited this fascinating country on seven different occasions, and each time I find myself becoming more intrigued by its culture, customs and people. Japanese life and activities move through age-long designs and patterns. Walking through the parks in Kyoto and exploring the lay-out of a Japanese garden, I was captivated by their simplicity, symmetry, beauty and balance. When I entered into a Japanese home, even the *tatami* (matted floor) is paved according to specifications. Homes are rarely cluttered; beds are simply rolled up and tucked neatly in a corner. *Ikebana*, the art of floral arrangement, is not something that you can pick up casually – it is a learnt art. Flowers have to be arranged in such a way that they blend with the space and the surroundings.

There are also rules for personal relationships. Harmony can be jeopardized by inadvertently giving the wrong signals or failing to interpret those given by the Japanese host. In business circles, the foreign businessman must ensure that he has an ample supply of business cards in both English and Japanese. Cards are presented with the left hand, after giving a slight bow with arms kept fairly straight, and palms pressed flat against the thighs. Body language such as eye-to-eye contact, so highly prized in Western countries, is often regarded as impolite by the Japanese. They prize personal space, which means that we *gaijin* (foreigners) should not move too close to them. Putting our arms around them or back-slapping is completely out of bounds.

The Japanese combine business with pleasure. They never like to see their guests tense and anxious. I was rather taken aback on my second visit to Japan when I suddenly realized that important business was discussed amongst Japanese men in the communal bath. The hot bath is a definite fixture in every Japanese home. I shall never forget my host offering me the first use of the heated bath. First I had to clean myself thoroughly with soap and water and then enter into a tank of hot water. The temperature gradually increased. I lasted twelve minutes and by then I felt like a boiled lobster! On my first visit my host diplomatically explained that no-one should ever pull out the bath-plug because it takes hours for the tank of water to reach such a high temperature. After my cares had been soothed away, then he and his family took turns to relax in that same bath.

I was amused to find out that there is a special way to wear the kimono. I have to wrap the left side of my kimono over the right side, because only corpses have their kimonos wrapped right over left!

It took me four visits to realize that when a

Japanese person nods his head, it does not mean that he is in full agreement with me. I must not decode it as a 'Yes', but simply as a recognition that I am being listened to politely.

We associate Japan with high-tech, and in many homes we will find sophisticated kitchen equipment, word processors, television sets with video recorders, and compact music systems. Offices are carefully computerized and in the mega-factories we will inevitably encounter robots. Japan leads the field in the development of artificial intelligence, and robotics is now a prestigious science.

Japan's modernity, especially in high technology, is balanced by its conservatism as far as tradition, culture and religion are concerned. Highly educated Japanese in their twenties still rely on the traditional system of *omiai*, the ancient Japanese term for marriage by arrangement, when it comes to selecting a mate. Although the Japanese are fully aware of Western courtship patterns, some find it very difficult to enter this world of *keikkon no ai*, or love-marriage.

I am told that parents still help their adult children to look for prospective marriage candidates. Through the intricate social network, word spreads quickly when a graduate of marriageable age is looking for a partner. Trusted acquaintances and relatives offer suggestions and then likely prospects have to submit their curriculum vitae (CV) or written résumés just like those used when applying for a job. In addition to these important papers, three photographs of the would-be partner are attached – the side-view and two full-face poses, preferably in traditional Japanese dress. Sometimes parents even employ private detectives to ferret out unsavoury characters. Once things are sorted out the couple can meet to discuss their life-goals and possible plans for their future together.

Japanese Christians normally pursue the route of arranged marriages. Here the pastor or student worker plays a vital role. Young adults can share their need for a partner and ask the pastor or staffworker to recommend a compatible partner. If they don't make such an approach, their concerned parents will. If an affirmative decision is made on both sides there is usually a period of a few months where both get to know each other.

When I once mentioned to a Japanese colleague about this ancient system existing side by side with modern technology, he coyly pointed out to me current Western innovations in computer dating and introduction services. These operate on the principle of finding the best match possible through careful pairing. *Omiai*, or arranged marriages, in Japan simply enable family and friends to be brought into the process, thus giving it a more secure, personal touch.

Workers in mourning

I remember once being taken to a gigantic factory in Kobe, Japan, where they were producing electronic parts. A number of workers were wearing black armbands but they were busily at work. I turned to my host and guide and asked him who had died. He smiled politely and assured me that no-one in this huge outfit had died, but that the people with armbands were workers who were on strike. He went on to explain, 'They are sad – you could say "in mourning" – because of their deep disagreements with the employers.'

What struck me was the genius of Japanese

management. True, there were differences between the employees and the management, but there was no loss of production. The plant kept on operating. The workers still earned their wages and at the same time they were involved in protracted negotiations with their bosses. How unlike strikes in other countries, where employees picket and shout 'Scabs!' at those who are prepared to return to work and who trade insults with their employers. These companies suffer because many man-hours have been wasted and the output diminished. Moreover, the morale of the company sinks to a low ebb, and customers become worried about whether their orders will be fulfilled or not.

What I saw that day made me reflect on the importance of maintaining good relations, even in the midst of conflict. As a result the good name of the company was not dragged into the mud.

Leading from the factory floor

I was intrigued when I visited a Chinese friend in Manchester. He was working on his PhD in Business Management and was studying the different styles of management in British and Japanese companies. The latter were all operating in England. He had been to several of the large British and Japanese conglomerates and was attempting to write his thesis from the viewpoint and perspective of the worker on the shop-floor. At first he was rather reluctant to share his findings because he still had to visit more plants and factories, but he gave me the following rather tantalizing observation. In the British companies he looked at, the managing director and his deputies worked in posh, comfortable offices. Parking spaces were reserved for their Jaguars or Daimlers. They had expensively decorated rooms where they could retire for a chat or a quiet smoke. They were pampered with cuisine served by a top-class chef. They had their own washroom facilities which no worker was allowed to use. It was a world of luxury and privilege which only they, the élite directors and managers, could enjoy.

By contrast, the Japanese managers donned overalls, ate in the same canteen as the workers, tried hard to appreciate English jokes and slang, shared the same washrooms and used the same car park with no special parking bays for directors and managers. So it was no surprise that the Japanese-managed companies tended to produce an *esprit de corps* which in turn resulted in greater productivity.

7

Out of South Africa

An honorary white in South Africa

'Honorary white' – that's how I was classified when I received my visitor's visa from the South African embassy in London. I smiled and wondered what rights this particular status would confer on me when I visited this complex racial, social and political country.

Within a day of my arrival I had a chance to test out my status. My host and I stopped at a petrol station. He was white and I was 'honorary white'. He told me that both of us could use the toilet facilities clearly designated 'Whites'. Out of curiosity I asked him whether I could also make use of the 'Non-Whites' facilities, and he nodded his head. So I went to that section as well. I think it is my one and only experience of visiting two different washroom facilities within a matter of five minutes!

I was appalled by the sharp contrast – the whites' facilities were immaculately clean, whereas the non-whites' section left much to be desired.

Two kinds of whites

My first major assignment was to speak at a conference for white English-speaking students. Many Christians at that particular camp were well aware of the gross injustice in their government's apartheid policies. They were, however, working for peaceful reforms.

A week later I visited two prestigious universities for the Afrikaans white students. These students traced their roots to their Dutch ancestors who emigrated to South Africa in the nineteenth century and achieved much as pioneers and nation-builders. The Christian students and staff at the universities of Potchefstroom (the Alma Mater of Afrikaans political leaders) and Stellenbosch were extremely polite and well-mannered and interacted intelligently with my expositions and talks. I found our dialogues, especially on social ethics, stimulating and illuminating. Although I agreed with most of their basic theological tenets, yet we differed radically when it came to the application of the gospel to society and racial equality. Their defence of apartheid was mainly based on history, sociology and very questionable biblical exegesis of racial superiority. I was surprised to learn that a number of theology students whom I met would one day be pastors of black reformed churches. They did not find it incompatible to be ministers of the gospel and at the same time to adhere to the principles and practice of apartheid.

Lunch at Parliament House

When I arrived in Capetown I was warmly welcomed by my host, Graham Mackintosh, who was then an Opposition Member of Parliament. He was formerly travelling secretary of the Student Christian Association. He had arranged for me to have lunch with Dr Connie Mulder, then the Minister of Internal Affairs. He was actively involved in the Broederbond, a powerful society which protected and preserved Afrikaans culture and language. He was also the enthusiastic architect who created homelands for various black groupings based on his racial separatist policies. When he knew that I was an international Christian leader he tried on a number of occasions to press home the point that his government adopted humane policies for black people. He maintained that they were better treated than blacks in other African countries. Dr Mulder then referred to his Christian beliefs and convictions. He and his family carefully observed the Lord's Day by regularly attending worship services and refraining from reading the Sunday papers.

I had learnt from experience never to challenge other people's beliefs and systems by publicly making moral judgments against their cherished positions; that only generates heated debate and makes my opponent extra-defensive. I was and am personally against apartheid because it contradicts the biblical doctrine of all men and women being made in the image of God.

So I began my verbal sparring with a question which honestly expressed my dilemma and puzzlement: 'Dr Mulder, I am glad to learn that you and your family are God-fearers and that you have such high moral standards. Would you agree that the greatest commandments for Christians to observe are to love the Lord our God with all our being and to love our neighbours as ourselves?'

His reply was prompt and firm, 'Of course, all

61

Christians believe that . . .'

'Dr Mulder, do you regard the blacks and coloureds in your country as your neighbours?'

He thought for a moment and then nodded his head in assent.

'Would you say that you love your black and coloured neighbours as yourself?'

He gave me a rather blank stare and said slowly, 'If you don't mind I would rather not answer that question.'

I am not sure whether he ever thought of that question again. For my part I was thankful that I had presented a prophetic question for him to answer.

Like me, Dr Mulder was also accountable to God.

Out they went and in they came

In Natal, Stuart Vaughan, the travelling secretary, drove me in his car to the University of Zululand. This was a tertiary institution for black students and on arrival the students were having their supper. On seeing us some began to boo and hiss. Stuart smiled and told me that I shouldn't get flustered, because that was the way in which they expressed their anger towards white people. Soon we met up with Sydney S.; he was the black travelling secretary and took us to a prayer meeting attended by a dozen students. They had publicized my arrival and the message that I would be giving that evening.

At around 7.45 p.m. there were about 200 students in the large hall. I spoke on 'The Gospel according to Marx and Mao – a Christian critique'. After speaking for about fifteen minutes a large number of students left their seats. I thought to myself, 'Surely I'm not such a dull and irrelevant speaker. After all, the topic is fairly exciting and the students themselves are listening attentively. Why the exodus?'

Sydney winked encouragingly and whispered rather loudly, 'They'll come back soon.'

I was even more puzzled. They couldn't all be rushing to the washrooms at the same time? I primed myself to speak to the remaining eighty or so students. Suddenly, students began streaming into the hall, and within a matter of minutes my audience had risen to over 600.

When I had finished speaking, and just before the question session was about to begin, one of the Christian leaders explained that black students sometimes turned up to meetings at which the speakers lectured on interesting topics, but turned out to be stooges of the government. They rarely heard independent speakers from abroad. Since what I had said did not toe the government line, I was worth hearing. Question after question was fired rapidly in my direction: What did I think of liberation theology? Would I agree that the blacks in South Africa correspond to the Israelites being oppressed by the Egyptians? Should Christians, like the Marxists, take up arms against their oppressors so as to regain their dignity and their land? Should Christians in other lands unite to fight against apartheid in South Africa?

It was clear that they wanted me to condemn and castigate their government. I agreed that the attitudes, policies and sins of their government were apparent, but at the same time the blacks should also admit to and repent of their sins. I quoted incidents of blacks hurting and killing blacks (these were in the days before the current hostilities between the Zulus, represented by the

Inkata Movement, and their adversaries in the African National Congress). I maintained that the oppressed had no right, especially if Christians, to exploit and hurt others. It was so easy to take the side of the underdogs, in this case the blacks, but then I would not have fulfilled my prophetic role as an ambassador of Jesus Christ.

Secret police must be evangelized too

Eleven years later, when I made my return visit to South Africa, I was primarily the guest of the Student Christian Movement – the evangelical movement for black students. I was the main speaker at their annual conference in Natal and we met in the renovated railway station. There were around 300 high school and college students and I was rather surprised that their songs and messages lacked the socio-political cutting edge.

Several whites were in the audience, some of them Christian students who wanted to express their solidarity with their black brothers and sisters. But there were four or five others who were in their late thirties or early forties and did not look like students. So I asked one of the black student leaders who those men were. He quietly announced, 'Secret police.'

I thought to myself, 'What a subtle way of keeping an international speaker off balance.' Their presence would make me more guarded in my messages. I had another problem. Usually when I prepare a message I have specific groups of people in mind, and I had not included members of the secret police force. So I had to send some arrow prayers heavenward for wisdom.

When I expounded the biblical passages, I

noticed that these police officers more or less switched off. When I began to apply Scripture to South African society and issues they listened intently. I told the audience real-life stories of persecutors who became Christians and stressed how the gospel transforms the lives of both oppressors and oppressed. So, instead of being put off by their presence, I was very thankful for this unexpected wider opportunity of sharing the gospel.

8

Corporate identity

Sweet-potato-vine evangelism

I once heard a Japanese pastor outlining his strategy on evangelism. He told his audience that he would never preach the gospel to an individual Japanese, but would always communicate the good news of Jesus to the whole family. This could be a long-term process. However, he testified that, in the long run, whole families were evangelized. He dubbed his approach as 'sweet-potato-vine evangelism'. Like a skilled farmer, his task was not just to cultivate the growth of an individual fruit, but to tend the vine so that it produces a cluster of fruits.

Meaningful relationships

I have always been fascinated by reading about or observing church growth in different countries. Whether it is in Chile or China or Cameroon, I have been struck by the simple but effective strategy of church-planting. It's true that the structures of some of these churches are rather authoritarian; the pastor or leader wields immense authority. So when he directs families in his church to go to another village or town to start a new congregation, they have to obey. They were, in reality, planting an instant church. Once they arrived in a new area, they would be found in the market place and, through the social web of relationships, they would testify to God's grace and invite people to hear more about their Lord and Saviour.

The secret lies in what I perceive as generation-to-generation evangelism. The Christians set up shops or are engaged in farm work. They relate and speak to their contemporaries. They share common interests and belong to the same generation. Men witness to men, women to women. Christian grandfathers sit in the village square and chat informally with other grandfathers. Christian grandmothers seek out neighbours who are also grandmothers. Christian children invite the children they meet at school and in the playground to participate in their Sunday school. Thus the gospel pervades the different age groupings of that town or village.

9

Family matters

Parental approval

It is very difficult for those of us who live and work in the West fully to understand corporate responsibility. A European or North American student can adopt his own distinctive lifestyle without consulting his parents. If he decides to change his religious affiliation he is free to do so, but this is not the case in the East. The great decisions of life — marriage, career and a change in religious faith — are rarely undertaken by the individual. He must first consult his parents and elders, for their acceptance and approval.

In September 1966, Leong Chee Loo was a final year Chemistry student at the University of Malaya. His cousin had invited him to an evangelistic mission. I can still recall vividly that sombre and heart-moving scene when he personally accepted the Lord Jesus Christ into his life.

Two nights later his cousin telephoned me. The message was crisp and clear, 'Chee Loo has been confined to his room by his father. He is absolutely mad at my cousin for becoming a Christian. He's given him an ultimatum: "Renounce your new faith or I will not support you through university."'

I was then a young student worker. My immediate wish was to leap into my car to drive straight to Chee Loo's home in Kuala Lumpur so that I could reason with his father and secure his release. But, as a Chinese, I realized that the older generation would only listen to their peers. So I contacted a well-known Chinese Christian doctor and a court interpreter (it was quite advantageous to invite him because he looked hefty and tough!). Together, we prayed and went to Chee Loo's home.

When we stepped into the living room, the atmosphere was quite tense. We introduced ourselves and my doctor friend explained to Mr Leong some misconceptions about being a Christian. For example, by becoming a Christian his son wasn't following a Western religion and Jesus Christ was not a European deity. Moreover, he was assured that Christians encourage young people to be loyal and kind to their parents and elders. Mr Leong listened politely, then, after a thoughtful pause, he turned and said to us, 'What you have said sounds reasonable. But I don't understand why you Christian preachers are always sharing your faith with our young people. Why don't you come first and talk to me? Why do you side-step the elders by going directly to our children? If I am convinced then my whole family can become Christians . . .' I have never forgotten those words of rebuke. Several years later, Mr Leong, his wife and all his sons and daughters committed their lives to Jesus Christ and are now actively involved in his Church. When I learnt about this in 1989, I asked Chee Loo to tell me the remarkable story of his family's conversion. As he shared, it was apparent that his life and consistent testimony had won over the members of his family. Since the year he was converted Chee Loo had always clung to the promise in Acts 16:31 – '"Believe in the Lord Jesus, and you will be saved – you and *your household*."'

Home-spun theology

Deuteronomy 6 provides an interesting setting for bringing up children. Theology is taught and caught in the home, not in the rarefied atmosphere of a theological seminary. We have found this to be true. As infants, all three of our boys were taught to thank God as they said grace in baby language. As they grew up, they saw us as parents relating to one another. Yes, there were times when we quarrelled and exchanged hard words, but they learnt to rejoice when we learnt to forgive and accept one another.

Our boys bickered too, but King Ling would never allow them to go to bed or to their rooms without making up. We were all very conscious of God's grace and forgiving love. When I wronged them I had to apologize, an almost impossible feat for a Chinese father (Chinese fathers are always right in front of their families!). Like us, our three sons learnt to exercise faith in a living God who cares and provides for our vacations, and gives extra funds to purchase a piano, a cello and a violin. Friends made holiday cottages available to us. Unexpected gifts from loved ones, plus the sale of part of a stamp collection brought in the extra funds for their instruments.

Theology often came to life at meal-tables and in bed. At the age of less than six years, Andrew and Daniel often asked profound questions about the

Trinity, the indwelling Christ and the new nature of the Christian. We once overheard Andrew commanding the indwelling Christ to come out of him so that he could see him personally!

When Daniel was eight he had to undergo surgery at Great Ormond Street Hospital in London. On the eve of his operation I saw him alone. We spoke and prayed together. I was naturally apprehensive (who isn't when surgery is involved?). Sensing my anxiety, he held my hand and said, 'Dad, you can go home now. Don't worry about me, because Jesus will take good care of me.' As I walked out of his ward that evening, tears were rolling down my cheeks. How thankful I was that God had become so real to Daniel.

Entertaining together

My job with IFES involved a fair amount of hospitality. We often entertained guests from different parts of the world. King Ling and I included our sons as co-hosts, and they helped us to prepare meals. Sometimes they would be responsible for making the fruit salad. Once they surprised us and our guests by serving half a water-melon creatively arranged like a turtle with raisins for the eyes. As they mixed with our international guests, they too broadened their cultural horizons. All three sons are avid travellers and Andrew is an international banker.

Some years ago, when I was abroad, a young couple came to seek out marital advice from King Ling. Both husband and wife had come from unhappy family backgrounds. They could hardly talk without arguing and shouting at one another. They almost came to blows, and King Ling found it extremely difficult to counsel them. At about 10 p.m. all three boys (their ages ranging from seven to twelve years), attired in their pyjamas, came into the room with three mugs of hot chocolate. They served their mother and the couple. They then gave King Ling a very warm hug and kissed her goodnight. The couple watched and suddenly both burst into tears. The loving and intimate ties between our sons and their mother presented a picture of what they had missed when they were children. They also recognized that as Christians there is hope in the God who is the source of love and secure relationships.

Family vacations

In 1974 heavy commitments in my work meant that I could only have a week of vacation with my family. In September that year when I visited Dr Oliver Barclay, who was then Chairman of the IFES Executive Committee, he asked me whether we had had a refreshing family vacation. I told him that I had only taken a week off. I thought that he would be impressed to see me making such sacrifices so that I could attend to the growing needs of the Fellowship. To my horror, he gave me a strong lecture; it was a dressing-down. He stressed that a week was much too short a time for any family to feel relaxed and urged me, where possible, to have at least a two-week stretch. That was wise counsel.

Looking back over the years, we have discovered how our family vacations have been high spots in our lives. King Ling and I have always been surprised that our boys prefer to go on family vacation with us even when in their twenties! Whether we were chatting, swimming, boating, fishing, cooking, playing Scrabble or simply enjoying the magnificent scenery around us, our vacations have brought us closer together and strengthened family bonds.

10

Story-telling

Tell us a story or two

A few months before his death, I was talking to Dr Francis Schaeffer in Lausanne, Switzerland.

I knew that Dr Schaeffer had often stressed the need for Christian apologists to underline propositional truths, so in our conversation I asked him what we should be doing if our present generation are no longer reading or engaged in logical thinking and reasoning. His reply was fascinating, 'I would tell them stories. That's the best way to lead them to consider spiritual truth.'

Our Lord did the same. To get the attention of his hearers he told them parables; short stories that made them think. Parables such as the Prodigal Son, the Good Samaritan, the Sower, the Rich Fool are compact, but packed with spiritual dynamite. They often provoke sharp responses.

I have been amazed in my international travels how eyes light up whenever I tell a story or relate an anecdote. In 1967 I wrote a modern parable, and in the ensuing years it has been reproduced and translated.

Two Trees: The Palm and the Mango

'Look at me, Mango Tree! Watch me sway in the
    evening breeze.'
Palm Tree was tall, slender and elegant; her
    figure graceful
as she bent before the summer winds.
Mango Tree was stocky; she could never boast of
    a graceful figure.
But she was a tree of wisdom.
'Be careful, Palm Tree,' she implored. 'Careless
    bending,
careless yielding will make you fall one day.'
'Life for me is to swing along,' answered Palm
    Tree, and Mango Tree was silent for a time.
Then she made another plea.
'Palm Tree, don't spread your roots too far out.
    Go deep.
Strike roots downward. Security lies in depth.'
'Who cares? The view is good up here, and
    besides, I want to go places.
Why bother with depth? Life is short.'
One day the skies darkened.
Thunder. Lightning. Fierce winds. Heavy rains.
A loud cry pierced the autumn storm.
Next morning brought bright skies, and cool
    breezes.
Mango Tree, firm as ever, looked down and
    mourned,
'Farewell, Palm Tree.
Life indeed is short.'

The Fox Hunter

As General Secretary of IFES, I used to edit a quarterly communiqué entitled *Priorities*. This was meant for the chief executive officers of our movements. I was delighted to receive a short note from Mr Soen Siregar, the Chairman of the Indonesian movement:

'Letters from IFES seldom catch my full undivided attention ... Your January 1989 *Priorities* was different. Possibly because it began with a very short letter.

'"Hey, it will only take one minute to read this *now*," I mused to myself. It was Saturday noon. The office was just closing. I relaxed ... and found myself reading the four pages through and through. Your story, "The Fox Hunter", stood out. Thank you for sharing this with us.'

I wrote that story because I wanted to draw the attention of decision-makers to the dynamics of committee work. I thought that ideological or propositional statements would simply result in a cursory glimpse, and that a story might be a better form of conveying my concern. Here it is.

Edward Foxhunter, 'E.F.' to his close friends, would not strike you as an impressive man. He wears thick glasses and sometimes appears lost in thought. But as you get to know him you will find that he is a very observant man. He will frankly confess that he uses both the rational and the intuitive approaches when analysing and · solving problems.

Catch for us the foxes,
*   the little foxes*
that ruin the vineyards,
*   our vineyards that are in bloom.*
                    (Song of Songs 2:15)

E.F. lives up to his name. He is an ecclesiastical fox hunter. When you examine his calling-card, you will see that he describes himself as a 'church-growth consultant' and, unlike other experts, E.F. will often spend three to four months in a church to help the pastor and leaders in resolving a wide variety of problems – spiritual, interpersonal and organizational.

You may wonder how I got to know E.F. in the first place. He was introduced to me by a fellow minister. I have been pastor of my church for nearly three years. It is a sound evangelical church with a membership of 150 adults, but when we include the children and occasional visitors, we reckon that we minister to around 300 people a week. I was glad that the majority of my council members gave me the go-ahead signal to see E.F. so that, after I was first appointed as pastor, we were able to fix dates for him to visit us.

When he arrived we arranged for an informal gathering, where various leaders in our church could get to know him. He was warm and witty; his nods and smiles encouraged people to speak freely. Throughout the week he attended our services and our meetings, and he had chats with our Sunday school teachers; he mixed well with our teenagers and they almost persuaded him to play a strenuous game of basketball with them!

At the end of his first month with us, he said in a rather casual fashion that he had identified a number of foxes in our church. I thought that this was rather strong language. But he assured me that he was just citing his text and mission – to hunt out foxes that would ruin God's work.

I had confided to E.F. that he could speak openly to two of our deacons and to myself. Our council had agreed that he should report to the three of us before meeting with the larger committee.

We were both apprehensive and excited to find out who the foxes in our church were.

His first 'fox' made us gasp in astonishment – Mr Good Intentions. After all, he is well known in Christian circles. He sits on various boards. He is eloquent and seems to support every good cause. But E.F. invited us to study his record. Yes, he has ideas. But he talks as if problems can be solved by platitudes and slogans. When we checked up on past minutes, we discovered that Mr Good Intentions was absent from more meetings than we had ever realized. Usually his secretary sent apologies for his absence. We had kept him on our council because of his fame, but the more we spoke to E.F. the more we were convinced that Mr Good Intentions was a liability.

E.F. spoke firmly, strongly recommending that we should discourage over-busy people from assuming positions of leadership. Less experienced leaders could be put on the council, who would be able to exercise a useful ministry as they learnt. E.F. advocated that we should bring into our leadership team people who were 100% behind the work.

We were not surprised when he named Mr Razor Sharp as another fox to be removed from our ranks. Mr Razor Sharp is extremely intelligent. His business associates describe him as the 'self-made' man. In any discussion he is the first to spot inconsistencies and he is not afraid to tear down other people's points of view. E.F. insisted, 'No, I am not suggesting that you should have 'Yes' men — or is it 'Yes' sheep? — on your committees.' The problem with Mr Razor Sharp is that he has such a penchant for shutting up members by his cutting words that they feel terribly uncomfortable with him and are unable to debate with him. His words can really wound and hurt fellow leaders.

If we are to give him the benefit of the doubt, I should lovingly confront him, so that it can be pointed out how he has been hindering God's work. I must confess that I have lacked the courage to speak the truth in love to Mr Razor Sharp. Leaders like him must learn to be sensitive and patient with others. Sharp and hurtful words do not build up team morale and partnership. I was convinced that if Razor Sharp did not repent, he should not be renominated for the next council.

We were taken aback when E.F. exposed Mr Ever Pleasing as a fox. 'Surely not Mr E.P.!' was the unanimous response. He is such a nice guy. You rarely see him sad or shaken. He is always smiling, easily mistakable for a Cheshire cat. Whenever there is trouble in the church or on the council he attempts to defuse any controversial issue. He refuses to face up to difficult problems. With his Eastern origins, he propounds the philosophy that we should never allow anyone to lose face. He thinks that it is unchristian to discipline others. 'We must love, love, love because love covers a multitude of sins.' It sounds spiritual, but we are aware that Mr Ever Pleasing and many other leaders often allow sin to fester. They are afraid to rebuke members who gossip and back-bite and those who embroil themselves in party struggles.

It occurred to us how difficult it is to get rid of nice guys like Ever Pleasing. But E.F. was swift to point out that if we allow weeds to grow in our garden, we will never be able to plant fruitful crops or beautiful flowers.

The fourth fox was Miss Negative. She sees problems in every proposal. She is always filled with fear. We noticed that several ventures of faith were curtailed because of her negative reactions. Sometimes we wonder whether the word 'faith' is in her vocabulary.

E.F. pointed out that it is important to have cautious people on our leadership team. They provide the necessary balance and check on those who are visionaries and tend to move much too quickly. Like a car, you need both the brake and the accelerator. But the problem with Miss Negative is that she breathes and breeds pessimism amongst leaders and members. Negative thinking can crowd God out of our plans. E.F. gently reminded us that only positive actions – based on clear conviction and goals, and exercised in faith – would produce growth.

Well, I mustn't bore you with the details of other foxes. E.F. says there are many little ones, who are nevertheless just as dangerous as the mature foxes.

Catching these foxes is an exacting task, but we will have to take definite action. I wonder what else Edward Foxhunter has in store for us?

11

Amazing love

Loving your enemy, even if it's Honecker

I shall never forget my first visit to East Germany in November 1981. After weeks of waiting I received a diplomatic visa and was considered an honoured guest of the state and church. My bags were not even checked when I presented them for customs clearance.

My first assignment was to speak at the student conference in Falkenberg. There I met Pastor Uwe Holmer, who was then the director of the Bible school. The Holmers had ten children. I learnt that the older ones could not get into university because they had publicly professed the Christian faith and at the same time refused to join the Young Marxists League. This meant that they had to compete for the tiny quota of places reserved for non-Marxists.

A month after my visit to East Germany, our family was over the moon when Andrew was accepted as a scholar at Pembroke College, Oxford.

After the euphoria I remembered Pastor Holmer and his children in East Germany and thought to myself, 'How would I have reacted if Andrew were rejected by his university simply because he was a committed Christian? How would I have advised him?' For us it was only a hypothetical situation, but for the Holmers, it was a grim reality.

In the autumn of 1989 East Germany was all over the papers and on our TV screens. The citizens of East Germany had marched against their government demanding freedom and reunification with West Germany. Soon the much-feared and hated president, Erik Honecker, was discredited. Amidst the social and political convulsions Pastor Holmer's name shot into prominence. I had almost forgotten him and it took me some time to recall that he was the same person that I had met in Falkenberg eight years previously. He had become the director of a Christian orphanage and of an old people's home. Pastor Holmer and his wife personally invited the Honeckers to stay in their family home. No other East German family would have extended their welcome to this infamous couple.

Mrs Honecker was the former Minister of Education. She initiated the policy giving special preference to young Marxists to study at university. She was therefore indirectly responsible for discriminating against the Holmer children. Yet the Holmers responded so differently. They could, together with their countrymen, have poured scorn and contempt on the disgraced ex-president and his wife. Instead, they opened their home and hearts to their 'enemies'.

Would I have done that? Not likely! I was simply dumbfounded by the actions of the Holmers. With tears in my eyes, I prayed, 'Lord, thank you for this demonstration of your amazing love.'

China – beauty from ashes

In September 1985, my wife and I, together with our two eldest sons, visited her ancestral village of Kwa Chiu, South China. One Sunday morning I sensed God saying to me, 'Go and make contact with my people in this village.'

King Ling had told me that when she was a child a Christian nurse had taken her to a small church – that was her first encounter with Christians. But we were not sure whether this person was still alive. When we made enquiries, King Ling's cousin told us all about Sister Q. She had suffered severe persecution and the church's property had been confiscated by the authorities and turned into a carpenter's shop.

After walking along narrow footpaths, we finally located the church and, next to the building, we met up with Sister Q. To King Ling's astonishment, she remembered her and was, of course, overjoyed to learn that we had come to love the Lord Jesus. She told us about her spiritual pilgrimage and every other sentence was punctuated by, 'Praise the Lord!' This was no pat cliché; she meant it. I watched her intently and I saw joy and peace shining through her wrinkled face. She wasn't bitter. She didn't complain. She exuded an air of serenity – the fragrance of someone who has been in the company of the Lord Jesus. She had certainly experienced 'the fellowship of his (Christ's) sufferings' (see Philippians 3:10).

What a joy it was to talk and listen to Sister Q. When we left her and the small group of believers, I was reminded of the Arab proverb, 'Crushed spices smell sweet.'

Iran – a bishop's prayer

I was tidying up some papers when I c aught sight of a prayer which a former colleague, John Ray of Pakistan, had sent to me. John himself had worked with students in Iran and was caught up in the thick of the uprising under the Ayatollah Khomeini. Whilst working in that country he got to know Bahram Dehqani-Tafti. Like John, Bahram was also a graduate of Oxford University. In the weeks that followed the revolution Bahram was tragically murdered.

His parents had to leave Iran and they relocated in Cyprus. In May 1980, Bishop Dehqani-Tafti penned this prayer:

A father's prayer
upon the murder of his son

O God
We remember not only Bahram but also his
*   murderers;*
Not because they killed him in the prime of his
*   youth and made our hearts bleed and our tears*
*   flow,*
Not because with this savage act they have brought
*   further disgrace on the name of our country*
*   among the civilised nations of the world;*
But because through their crime we now follow
*   Thy footsteps more closely in the way of*
*   sacrifice.*
The terrible fire of this calamity burns up all
*   selfishness and possessiveness in us;*
Its flame reveals the depth of depravity and
*   meanness and suspicion, the dimension of*
*   hatred and the measure of sinfulness in human*
*   nature;*

It makes obvious as never before our need to trust
in God's love as shown in the Cross of Jesus
and His resurrection;
Love which makes us free from hate towards our
persecutors;
Love which brings patience, forbearance,
courage, loyalty, humility, generosity,
greatness of heart;
Love which more than ever deepens our trust in
God's final victory and His eternal designs for
the Church and for the world;
Love which teaches us how to prepare ourselves
to face our own day of death.
O God,
Bahram's blood has multiplied the fruit of the
Spirit in the soil of our souls;
So when his murderers stand before Thee on the
day of judgement
Remember the fruit of the Spirit by which they
have enriched our lives,
And forgive.

12

More than words

They speak our language

When television first came to Singapore in the early sixties there was naturally great excitement. One day when I was visiting my parents' home, my grandmother, who was then in her seventies, was watching *Tarzan*. It was an old movie with Johnny Weissmuller as lord of the jungle. The sound-track was dubbed in Chinese. My grandmother turned to me and exclaimed, 'These Americans and Africans are extremely intelligent. They speak our language!'

I didn't want to spoil her enjoyment of the film and so I simply nodded and smiled.

There is nothing more boring, I suppose, than having to watch a film or listen to a talk in an unintelligible language. As a communicator, my passionate concern is that my audience can understand my message. This means that often on my travels I am highly dependent on interpreters. If they translate well my audience hear my message in their own language.

Speaking through an interpreter demands discipline. If I were to develop a point in lengthy sentences I could easily lose my interpreter. That reminds me of the story of an American general during the Korean war. He was addressing South Korean troops and he was carried away when relating a rather humorous anecdote. He must have spoken for about ten minutes. The Korean interpreter gave a one-sentence interpretation and everyone laughed. The general was surprised but continued his address. Afterwards, back at the mess, the American general took his interpreter aside and asked, 'How come you were able to interpret my long story in one sentence and everyone laughed?'

The reply was terse, 'I simply told the men, "The general has cracked a joke. Everyone please laugh."'

More than words

In February 1983 I was speaking at a small Baptist Church in Santiago, Chile. My Chilean pastor-host invited a young American missionary to translate for me. I sensed that he did this fairly well; his words flowed smoothly and swiftly, and he did not falter throughout the whole sermon. Afterwards I asked my host, Josué Fonseca, for his assessment of my interpreter. He shook his head and muttered, 'Not good, not good!'

I pressed him, 'Was he not accurate in his interpretation?'

'He was very accurate. But he didn't translate well because when you were waving your arms and moving around, he was standing still. That's not Latin!'

So I discovered that you have to throw yourself passionately into your preaching, whether you are the preacher or the interpreter.

Experts in communication tell us that there are twenty gestures that English or Chinese preachers normally utilize, while the Latins have 200!

Interpreters rule OK

I remember preaching at a Presbyterian Church in Mexico City in January 1982. My good friend, Pablo Perez, was my interpreter. I was expounding Luke 14, and my theme was the cost of discipleship. I noticed that he was putting more rev and roar into my sermon than I was, and the audience was visibly moved. As I concluded I invited him to lead in prayer, but he stopped me. He asked me to sit down and relax. For five minutes he continued to preach with tremendous fire and zeal, challenging folk to stand to indicate their commitment to Jesus Christ. And many responded.

After the service I thanked Pablo for being so sensitive to what we both discerned was the moving of the Spirit. Pablo hugged me and said, 'God was speaking so powerfully through your exposition that it would have been unforgivable not to issue a summons to follow the Lord Jesus.'

In Madagascar too

The university auditorium at Antananarivo was jammed with 2,000 students on 1 March 1991. It was the annual evangelistic rally of the GBU. The entire meeting lasted three hours and forty-five minutes but the audience was not bored. They enjoyed the music and drama. I was to preach on the return of Jesus. Daniel Rakotojoelinandrasana, a medical doctor and Chairman of the Malagasay movement, was my interpreter. We both sensed the power of the Holy Spirit and, as agreed, he was to make the appeal. My role was to present Christ from the Scriptures, but because he was fully at home with the culture and mind-set of the hearers, he was in a better position to challenge the students to commit themselves. What a harvest! Over 200 stepped forward to commit their lives to Christ.

Tears speak louder

I was once invited to give a series of talks on world mission to an ethnic church in California. It was a fairly large congregation and most of its members were affluent. The annual missions budget was close to US $200,000. The pastor and the missions committee were very concerned because for the last five years only one family from their church had responded to the missionary call to serve as cross-cultural ambassadors for Christ. Somehow I felt that my hearers were thinking, 'It's great that some people are willing to give their lives for cross-cultural missions, but it's not for me. I don't mind making a substantial financial contribution to support our church's missionary programme.' Some on the missions committee even intimated that if they could raise half a million dollars in pledges they would be satisfied. But I liked the faithful spirit of the chairman: 'We must have six people offering themselves for missionary service this year.'

On the final night I spoke on the plight of the

lost and described the awfulness of being separate from a holy, loving God. The reality of hell dawned upon us all. There was a hushed silence. I began my next sentence and as I looked at my interpreter, she was in tears. She couldn't interpret.

I had to make a decision. I could ask for another interpreter and so continue my message, or I could wait. I chose the latter. And those ninety seconds of silent but pensive interlude probably spoke to more hearts than I had anticipated. Today that interpreter and her husband are serving the Lord as 'tent-making' missionaries. I learnt that four others have also yielded their lives for missionary service. I wonder whether this would have taken place without my interpreter's tears.

13

Tales of the unexpected

Dog-bite evangelism

We first met Sashi at a staff conference in Southern India. She is the wife of Jebaraj, and together they seek to share the gospel of Jesus Christ with students in the Indian state of Orissa. One day, whilst Jebaraj was away visiting scattered Christian Unions, Sashi decided to venture into a nearby university town. Armed with invitations, she decided to invite as many Hindu students as possible to attend a special seekers camp. She had wanted to mobilize some of the Christian students to assist her in distributing these invitations, but they were away at their classes, so she had to walk alone in the sweltering heat from hostel to hostel, enthusiastically promoting the conference. The results were meagre; she received several polite responses of 'I'll think about it', which she knew meant, 'I'm not coming.'

Feeling discouraged, she prayed that God would give her a breakthrough. Little did she guess what would be in store for her! Suddenly, a stray dog ran straight at her and bit her. She froze with fear, as she saw blood spurt out; she wondered whether she had caught the dreaded rabies. Several medical students rushed to her aid and carried her to a nearby student lounge. They washed and dressed her wound. Soon there was a growing bond between Sashi and this group of students. They asked her why she had come to their town, which provided an ideal cue for Sashi to explain her mission. Question after question followed and she shared her spiritual pilgrimage, relating how she had started life as a Hindu but had never found this age-old religion satisfying. She went on to tell how she met the living Christ.

As a result of that unexpected encounter, five of the Hindu medical students attended the seekers camp and two were wonderfully converted. This must be a rare case of dog-bite evangelism!

Stoned for the gospel?

My friend Nigel Lee was once leading an evangelistic team for Operation Mobilisation. They had driven their truck to an Indian town, where they sang and preached in the open air. This met with a hostile reaction and soon some men from the crowd were pelting them with rocks and stones. When a riot was about to erupt, Nigel shouted instructions to his team members to jump aboard and ordered the driver to start the engine and accelerate hard.

Half an hour later the team stopped by a cafe to nurse their wounds and hurt pride. Whilst sipping their welcome cups of hot tea, they watched two young men on a motor-scooter arrive at the cafe. One of them immediately approached Nigel and asked, 'Were you the people who were preaching in our town earlier in the day?'

'Yes,' Nigel replied, rather cautiously.

'Then we would like to know more about your God and your religion. There must be something real and worthwhile about your faith, otherwise why did you court such suffering?'

Before long, both young men professed faith in Christ. God's ways and thoughts are often above ours.

£10,000 sermon

It's always very difficult for me to know which speaking engagements to accept whenever I am in England. I thought that I should respond positively to a small missionary college that was holding its annual graduation service. As expected, it was a warm meeting of friends and supporters of the college and I expounded the Scriptures for about half an hour.

Later an older man walked up to me to thank me for my message. He introduced himself as the secretary of the trust which I had contacted a few weeks previously, soliciting a grant for a training project. With a wink in his eye he said to me, 'Brother, you should expect to receive a cheque from us next week.' Three days later in the post there was a cheque for £10,000.

I reflected on this extraordinary provision. I was very glad that I had made the right decision to preach at the missionary college. That choice was not governed by the size of the audience. It also dawned on me the importance of personal face-to-face encounters. Had that trustee not met me and heard me, would the trust have responded so generously?

Talking of unexpected gifts, my mind flashed back to a scene in the sitting-room of a well-to-do missions supporter. She was most hospitable and kind, and listened courteously to my presentation. When the time came for me to leave for my next engagement I thanked her for her thoughtfulness, and she asked me to sign her guest book; I was pleased to oblige. I noticed that she was watching me intently as I wrote my name and address with my Schaeffer pen. 'I am very pleased that you are writing with a fountain pen with real ink,' she said. 'I must increase my giving to your Fellowship.'

I was rather taken aback and asked her, 'Forgive me for asking, but why did you decide to increase your giving to IFES simply because I have an ink pen?'

'Oh, most people today write with these disposable pens called biros or whatever. They don't take much pleasure in their writing. I always reckon that people who use good fountain pens are those who believe in continuity and stability.'

The Lord hid my passport

I would like you to meet Sergio. He is a lecturer in Education in Cochabamba, Bolivia. He spends most of his free time visiting the student groups in his city; he is a part-time staffworker. I met him in Quito, Ecuador, at an IFES new staff training conference in February 1990.

Together with fourteen other new student workers, he was in this high altitude city for ten weeks of intensive training. After sitting through four weeks of Bible teaching, and learning all he could about the distinctive principles of student work, Sergio and another trainee were asked to travel to Colombia to spend two or three weeks working with a local Christian Union.

They boarded the crowded bus, replete with passengers, chickens, ducks, dogs and piglets. Sergio and his companion chattered openly with their fellow passengers. As they were approaching the Colombian border, their passports had to be checked. Sergio fumbled in the pockets of his jacket and rummaged through his rucksack, but couldn't find his passport. The immigration police summoned him to leave the bus so that they could interrogate him.

For one hour a junior officer questioned him, 'What are you doing in our country?' Sergio told him truthfully that he had been in Quito to learn all he could about how best to share the good news of Jesus with students. The officer said, 'Then you must be an evangelical.' Sergio nodded.

'You have no passport, but surely you must have a Bible. Please let me see it.'

Sergio handed his Spanish Bible to the officer, who flipped rapidly through its pages. Shaking his head he claimed, 'You're not an evangelical. All evangelicals underline their Bibles, but yours isn't underscored at all!'

Poor Sergio had to convince the officer that there were other ways of studying the Scriptures.

'All right, all right,' said the officer. 'I am convinced that you are a believer, a good evangelical Christian. But since you don't have a passport, I must take you to see my chief. Wait here while I go and talk to him.'

Within a few minutes he returned and escorted Sergio to the office of the chief immigration officer. With folded arms and sitting regally in his plush chair, this senior officer announced, 'I have been waiting for you for a long, long time.' Before

Sergio could regain his composure, the officer proceeded to tell his life story, speaking of his personal problems and the guilt he felt for the terrible things he had done. His marriage was on the rocks. Could God help him sort out this mess? Could there really be forgiveness in spite of all his sins? How does one find God these days?

For over an hour Sergio chatted with the officer and pointed him to various parts of the Scriptures, reassuring him that God in Christ seeks out men like him. Finally, the officer indicated that he would like to receive the Lord Jesus into his life. Both men prayed and there was great rejoicing.

The officer then said to Sergio, 'I am so grateful to you for introducing me to Jesus Christ, but I'm afraid that I still can't let you go to Colombia without a passport. Let me see whether my police training can help you locate your passport ... I'd like you to empty your rucksack and the pockets of your jacket and trousers.'

They went through Sergio's belongings with a fine-tooth comb. As they were about to give up, the police chief's eye caught a glimpse of a brown folder.

'What's in that file?'

'Oh, nothing, just some papers and a notebook.'

'Open it anyway.'

He did so, and out fell the passport.

Later, when all the trainees reassembled in Quito, sharing what they had learnt, Sergio's testimony was arresting:

'I believe the Lord hid my passport so that I could witness to the police chief.'

14

To Russia with love

Bible barter

Mikhail Gorbachev, the former President of the Soviet Union, has often been described by believers in his country and outside as a modern Cyrus. His policies of *glasnost* and *perestroika* meant that the gospel could be proclaimed more openly in this vast country.

The Operation Mobilisation ship, *Logos II*, paid a historic visit to Leningrad in July 1990. The deputy mayor of the city performed the opening cere-mony, where thousands flocked to browse and buy books. Leaflets and tracts which were distributed by the OM team were carefully kept and read.

When the time came for the ship to pay for its mooring fees the authorities informed the captain that they did not wish to receive any roubles but would like to be paid in hard currency or Bibles. The full payment of port dues amounted to forty Russian Bibles!

Sent to Siberia

During the Cold War years, Siberia was a synonym for exile, hard labour and extinction. I was surprised to discover that the key Siberian city, Novosibirsk, exercises tremendous influence over Russian youth culture, setting the pace for fashion and music. Novosibirsk beats with the pulse of youth culture.

Siberia is also famous for Akademgorodok, the élitist scientific institution. About 100,000 live on this unique campus, which has been described as the world's biggest think-tank. This university was also notorious for its atheism.

It is indeed remarkable that each week around 150 people at Akademgorodok gather to study the Bible. Nearly all are not even Christians but are attracted by the Scriptures. How thrilled we were to be able to send a team of three to give a week-long series of lectures on the Christian faith.

On arrival, Jonathan Lamb (the IFES European Regional Secretary), Jürgen Spiess (General Secretary of the Studenten Mission in Germany) and his co-worker, Hartmut Zopf (formerly General Secretary of the Studenten Mission in the German Democratic Republic), were interviewed and interrogated live on the Siberian State Radio. It was a 'no holds barred' session. The programme's producer had, in fact, written two books lambasting the Christian faith. He came to realize that his scathing attacks were groundless and even made an open statement to that effect on the air!

Stimulating questions followed the lectures and both staff and students requested Bibles and literature.

Wheat and weeds

This new climate of openness in what is now the Commonwealth of Independent States and in Central Europe provides fertile ground for the cults and the New Age movement. To see Polish Hare Krishna devotees chanting, singing and dancing on the main shopping street in Warsaw, surrounded by milling crowds, was an unforgettable sight. The Mormons opened an office next to the Bible Society, and the Jehovah's Witnesses volunteered to repaint a football stadium so that they could hold four nights of public rallies there; these drew crowds of over 60,000.

In Siberia itself thirty Mormons were busy distributing attractive Russian translations of the Book of Mormon.

In the republic of Estonia, Transcendental Meditation is proving extremely popular and a Maharishi Ayurveda university is being established in Tallinn.

This surely demonstrates that tares and weeds spring up alongside the fruitful gospel seed. It challenges believers really to know their Lord and their faith in order to discern and combat spurious teaching.

Only in English?

I was surprised to discover that several youth groups in the big cities in the former USSR run their meetings in English. The Christians who initially encouraged Soviet students to come together were English-speaking, as were their songs and their style of operation. It came as a breath of fresh air, therefore, when a colleague exhorted them to share and communicate their faith and to develop their groups in Russian.

We call the shots

Pete Lowman, an IFES colleague, was once speaking at a dormitory of a Soviet State University. The authorities agreed to sponsor the meeting but wanted to call the shots regarding the programme. They reckoned that it was appropriate to follow up Pete's talk with a 'religious film'. So the film chosen for the evening was 'Jesus Christ Superstar'. Pete confessed, 'I would most certainly not have made that my choice for the first meeting of IFES in this university. However, I might not have been preaching to 200 students if that film had not been shown.'

15

Food, glorious food

Jesus enjoys a good supper

Some years ago, when I was seeking to lead a fellow-student from Singapore to Christ, I directed him to Revelation 3:20: 'Here I am! I stand at the door and knock. If anyone hears my voice and opens the door, I will go in and eat with him, and he with me.' The Authorized Version translated 'eat' as 'sup'. When I asked my seeker friend what he thought the last part of the verse meant, he was quiet for about a minute and then exclaimed excitedly, 'If I invite Jesus into my life, he wants to be my life-long companion – my special friend.'

'That's right. But what made you say that?' I asked.

'Well, Jesus said that he will sup with me and I with him. Supper is never a rushed meal and you can only enjoy your dinner with someone whom you regard as a close friend.'

He was so thrilled at his own discovery that there and then he invited Jesus into his life.

With tongue in cheek, I sometimes say to my

audience, 'Luke's Gospel is a Chinese gospel, because Luke records Jesus' presence at seven parties or banquets.' He was accused of enjoying food and special feasts.

In the East, the worst thing that could happen to anyone would be for his guests at table to turn against him. Jesus expressed his deep sadness when Judas decided to betray him. He cited Psalm 41:9: ' "Even my close friend, whom I trusted, he who shared my bread, has lifted up his heel against me" ' (see John 13:18).

Sorry, no Maori restaurants

The French and the Chinese are very proud of their cuisine, so in most cities of the world you can dine in a Chinese or French restaurant.

In August 1984 I was in Auckland, New Zealand and had three free hours. At lunchtime I thought I would sample the local fare and instantly my mind registered the message 'Try Maori food', so I walked briskly to the nearest Tourist Information Bureau and asked the receptionist where I could find a Maori restaurant. She stared at me blankly, and I thought that I must have mispronounced 'Maori'. I repeated myself, and then she shouted rather excitedly to her manageress, much to my embarrassment, 'This gentleman wants to eat Maori food. Is there a Maori restaurant here in the city?'

Both stared at me rather incredulously, and I felt a little hot under the collar. Finally, the manageress said, 'If you join a special excursion to a Maori settlement or village, they do have a special roast ham that they cook buried in the earth. That's delicious. But unfortunately there is no Maori restaurant.'

Fish and chips in Nigeria

During my initial trips to Africa, I sensed that my hosts always seemed to be nervous and cautious about food. Imagine my disappointment when my student hosts at the university of Lagos, Nigeria, specially brought me fish and chips for my supper! They had learnt that I had come from London and that fish and chips was the national dish of the British, therefore I would appreciate their gesture. At the next main meal, when they ordered fish and chips, I protested because I had intimated that I would like to eat something local. One of the lady students asked, 'Do you mean that you would like to eat plantain (fried banana)?' I nodded. Later, one of the students who had got to know me better told me why they had decided to buy me fish and chips. Apparently, the week before my visit the table-tennis team from Mainland China had been giving a series of exhibition matches in Lagos. They had undiplomatically criticized the local food. Since I was Chinese, my Christian friends were afraid that I too would be put off by local food.

I am very grateful that the Lord has given me an international stomach. Since I was brought up in Singapore I had experienced the best cuisine from East and West. I was able to eat hot and spicy food, and that put me in a very favourable position when I ate with my Korean colleagues. Since it was my first visit to Seoul, their capital city, they were sizing me up and wondering how I would react to their food and customs. They were absolutely astonished when I relished their *kim chi*, a hot, spicy Chinese leaf marinated in vinegar. When I consumed vast quantities of red chilli pepper they roared with laughter, remembering American and

European missionaries who had had to yell for cold water when they had accidentally eaten some of it.

Some of my co-workers find it extremely difficult to savour exotic food, so they have to resort to the famous missionary prayer:

'Lord, where Thou leadest I would follow,
What Thou givest, I would swallow.'

Caterpillars

I shall never forget going to a market in Harare, Zimbabwe, with Roy Musasiwa. We went to a local market and in one section the meat, fruit and vegetables were for European consumption. I wanted him to take me to a section where I knew only the local folk would go shopping. So I begged Roy to guide me to the stalls that sold local products. He obliged and soon we stopped at a stall. There was a huge aluminium tray and wisps of smoke and steam rose from what I though was a pile of boiled ground nuts. Roy turned to me and said, 'Hey, Wee Hian, you may want to try this. These are boiled caterpillars. In Shona it is called *harati*, or, in another dialect, *madora*.'

'Surely you can't eat them?' I challenged Roy.

'Of course you can,' he replied. 'These caterpillars, in fact, contain more protein than anything I know.'

He spoke to the lady and I saw him popping a few of these boiled caterpillars into his mouth. 'Would you like some?' he asked me, rather cheekily. I politely declined.

Pet food

Once when I was with our Latin American staff team at a training conference for new workers in Quito, Ecuador, I was told that the conference centre, which was located in a government husbandry station, specialized in the production of an exotic kind of meat. My colleagues did not have the English word for it. Anyway, my Latin American Regional Secretary, Dieter Brepohl, smiled and said, 'Our IFES conference budget cannot afford this meat.' I was very curious. One day Dieter told me that I could find these animals being bred in a special shed across from our conference building. I immediately rushed into this huge wooden shed and as I opened the door I saw thousands of guinea-pigs! They were of Abyssinian stock. I once gave them as pets to our sons. The thought that these beautiful animals were prized for their meat made me feel sick. So I was very glad that we couldn't afford this item on the menu!

Roast puffins

Equally, when a journalist took me to a restaurant in Reykjavik, Iceland, two items were offered as the meat of the day – roast puffins and red snapper fish. Since I love watching birds, and had enjoyed the strange gait and movements of the puffin, my choice was a simple one – red snapper fish.

Soul food

Whilst on the subject of food, I have always been impressed at the way in which students who operate coffee bars or invite their friends to simple meals find that their guests are more receptive to the gospel in such an informal and cordial atmosphere. In 1960, when our local church had the unique experience of witnessing over a hundred students becoming Christians, I once said to the pastor, 'Do you know that more folk commit their lives to Jesus Christ after they've been to one of our evangelistic suppers, than at the evangelistic services that we run on Sundays?'

My old pastor smiled and said, 'Don't you know that the way to a man's heart is often through his stomach?'

The goat's for you

We are used to buying our meat neatly cut up and packaged and then adding spices, salt, pepper and flour to create our favourite meat dish.

In February 1991, I was staying on the farm of the chairman of the Tanzanian student movement, Chuwa Eliapenda. He was a most generous and courteous host. As I was the guest of honour, in accordance with Tanzanian hospitality, he announced that he was giving me one of his goats. Half an hour later one of his servants dragged out a reluctant spotted he-goat; that was my gift. I thanked Chuwa. Then, in a rather matter-of-fact tone, he announced, 'That goat will provide dinner for the council members, my family and for you tonight.' The poor creature was led away bleating. My IFES colleague, Samuel Are, of Nigeria, was given the honour of slaughtering and dressing the goat for me. It was too late to declare that I would prefer to be a vegetarian (at least on that occasion!).

I hurried away to another corner of the farm, so that I would not hear or see the poor goat being killed. I also came to the solemn conclusion that I probably would not make it as a local travelling secretary because of my squeamishness at having to kill a live animal!

16

Travel and transportation

Airports

Airports are usually centres of noise and activity. The PA systems announce flight departures: 'This is the final call for flight CX213 for ... Will passengers ... and ... identify themselves at departure gate number 9.' In the departure terminal itself you can see passengers anxiously gazing at TV monitors to make sure that their flights are leaving on schedule, or at the rescheduled time. They become increasingly worried when no gate numbers appear next to their flight numbers.

Stress and strain are no strangers to airports. I have seen breathless passengers perspiring profusely and getting very nervous as they queue up for their check-ins. Sometimes in their anxiety to rush to the departure lounge as soon as possible, they leave behind their tickets and passports.

Heathrow, the world's busiest airport, is where I often board planes for my international journeys. It is always tempting to look at the rows of newly published books. The top thrillers are always well advertised: Stephen King, Danielle Steel, Victoria Holt, Jeffrey Archer – these writers seem to churn out best-sellers. I sometimes try to make a mental calculation of the royalties that they will earn from the sale of their popular books.

I usually make my way to the racks that display management books. Success, efficiency and productivity are boldly highlighted on their covers. I flip through some of the titles and notice catchy chapter headings, humorous anecdotes and true-to-life case histories. Ultimately, it is the effective communicator who tips the balance and forces me to purchase his book.

Plane journeys can be tedious or enjoyable. I spend most of my time reading light magazines or a newly acquired management book, and when I get tired I work on crossword puzzles. I enjoy the in-flight entertainment, since I don't normally watch the local movies. These specially edited films often reflect the morals and life-perspectives of people today. I notice heads nodding when in my sermons I refer to the painfulness of divorce as portrayed in *The War of the Roses*, or the mixed-up morality of *Pretty Woman*. I am glad that passengers are also given fairly up-to-date newscasts. I doubt if I shall ever forget my flight between Singapore and Manila on 27 December 1989. There, on my in-flight screen, I saw the slumped bodies of the dictator Nikolai Ceauçescu and his wife.

Some of my colleagues suffer from severe jet lag. They have tried all kinds of formulas – eating only certain foods at certain times, avoiding alcohol at all costs, and sitting in certain postures. But in almost every case they succumb to jet lag. Today I still cannot fathom why I suffer so little from it. On long flights where there is a time difference of more than seven hours I normally take four to eight hours to recover. I try not to think of the time zone that I have left behind. I am very thankful to God for my unusual biological clock which seems to adapt so quickly to changing time zones.

Big business corporations do not allow their executives to sign important agreements after a long journey. They have to rest for at least twenty-four hours before they can negotiate and then sign important papers. I wish I could afford this luxury! I am often hauled directly from the airport to speak at a meeting. Because I am an international speaker, my audience have high expectations. I am amazed at the number of times I bounce back from physical tiredness. I have proved the promise of 2 Corinthians 12:9: '"My grace is sufficient for you."'

Wandering around

In the midst of a tight, packed programme, I often ask my host for permission to wander around by myself. I enjoy savouring the atmosphere – the colour, the smell and the noise of people buying and selling at the local markets. Seeing people haggling over the price of a bunch of bananas or a live chicken reminds me of the days when I had to do the same in the markets of Singapore and Hong Kong. I make a mental note of the prices, especially of basic cereals and rice. To maintain a well-balanced diet I always buy local fruits.

In August 1988 when I was in Lomé, Togo, I word-sketched the following scenes:

It is quite an unforgettable experience to visit the open market in Lomé. The streets are narrow, crowded with stalls. Huge umbrellas and parasols provide shade for the stall-keepers. On round or square wooden tables there is a large variety of merchandise — cosmetics, household utensils, shoes, textiles. Competing with these stall-keepers are the itinerant vendors who also display their wares and advertise their goods.

One young girl has a bale of colourful cloths finely balanced on her head. She tries enthusiastically to sell a long piece of material with new patterns on it to an eager customer. Nearby, a male vendor, probably in his early twenties, has between thirty and forty bras resting on one arm. With the other I see him thrusting a black bra into the hand of a matronly woman. She shakes her head and tries to walk away, but he, undaunted, produces a green one. There isn't the slightest trace of embarrassment and he persistently continues to approach every woman who crosses his path.

Oops! I have to tread carefully. It's quite easy to trip over open aluminium pots filled with lemon drink or murky brown milk coffee, heavily sugared. I can see the slabs of ice floating in these containers. Flies in their hundreds settle on the rims of the pots. My stomach churns and I cannot imagine myself sampling these cold drinks. I walk on and watch a group of woman foraging through piles of synthetic and inexpensive jewellery. They shout and barter with the vendor. I notice their colourful dresses. Most of them are wearing flowing dresses, African style. But the men sport batik shirts and western jeans.

I am fascinated by the ladies' hairstyles. African coiffure is a work of art. There are distinctive styles, but nearly all are braided and covered with an attractive head-dress.

Amidst the cacophony of sounds the vendors are shouting and vying with their rivals to attract customers. Suddenly, a hen escapes into the crowd and soon half a dozen boys are pursuing it. Shrieks, cackles and screams follow. There is temporary pandemonium.

Suddenly, I find a dark hand descending on my wrist. Nothing to fear, it's a friendly invitation to view watches from Hong Kong, Taiwan and Switzerland.

Looking foreign, I'm the natural object of interest to money-changers. They thrust bundles of 100 franc notes in my face and promise me unbeatable rates for my dollars or Deutschmarks. I hear music — Western pop songs. I see a large crowd gathering because a band with a full complement of drummers is in full swing producing joyful notes. As I walk in the direction of the music I realize that I am approaching the compound of a large Catholic church. It's a wedding. The bridegroom, resplendent in his headgear, and his radiant bride are marching out into the courtyard. They are surrounded by a swarming multitude of relatives, friends and well-wishers.

Across the street I witness a different scene. This time I hear drums and gongs. Within seconds men dressed in white prostrate themselves on the ground, facing east. These are Muslim merchants and they are responding to the hour of prayer, when they face Mecca and worship Allah. What a spectacle of religious devotion!

This is paradise

In 1966 when I was living and working in Malaysia, I remember a Burmese driver in Kuala Lumpur asking me for directions to a local bank. Then, with an ecstatic gesture, he raised his voice and exulted, 'This is paradise! This is paradise!' When he saw

112

my bewildered look, he explained apologetically that in Rangoon, Burma, the roads were so poorly maintained, it was very difficult to drive on them. The well-paved roads of Malaysia were like highways in paradise compared with the roads in his country.

Human milk shake

In 1982, on my first visit to Kampala, Uganda, the student movement's General Secretary, David Zac Niringiye, had to navigate the movement's VW minibus around huge craters. Often he had to skirt around villages and small towns on dirt tracks, travelling on a bumpy, untarred road. It made me feel like a milk shake; but I remember giving thanks to God for steady, German-made shock absorbers, which made my journey less treacherous.

Rickshaws – human degradation?

When I first visited Hong Kong in December 1962, after spending nearly six years in England, I found myself feeling rather ashamed and embarrassed when my host invited me to ride on a rickshaw. The driver was running with tattered canvas shoes in the pelting rain. For his hard labour he earned only a few cents. As I sat on the Star Ferry crossing the harbour from Hong Kong to Kowloon, I questioned myself. Why did I feel guilty? Wasn't the rickshaw driver glad to earn those extra cents? It suddenly dawned on me that I had a different concept of the value of human beings. That driver was made in the image of God, and for me it was humiliating that another human being should use his physical strength to cart me from one place to another. When I learnt that many of these rickshaw drivers die young of consumption, I felt even sadder. I am glad that in the early sixties the Hong Kong government banned this form of transportation except for tourist joy-rides.

Clear the buffaloes off the runway

I looked at my watch and it was 4.50 p.m. Soon we would be landing at Bacolod City, Philippines. Two minutes later the pilot announced to the passengers sitting comfortably in the Fokker Friendship plane that we would be landing in five minutes. I peered through the window and realized that we were circling around a small airfield. We were only a few hundred feet above the ground, so when the pilot announced that there would be a delay of several minutes before the plane would land, my heart missed a few beats. I looked through the window again and, to my horror, there was a large herd of water buffaloes on the runway. Two uniformed guards were trying to chase these animals away but some were not being very co-operative. More airport employees were mobilized and joined in the effort to herd the buffaloes away from the airfield. With a great sigh of relief we landed safely and taxied towards the terminal. I checked my emotions. There was relief and joy that we had been able to reach our destination safely, but also anger that the airport authorities had endangered our lives by not taking adequate precautions against these beasts ambling on to the runway.

Getting through customs

Getting through customs can sometimes be a tedious task. After a long wait, you come face to face with an immaculately dressed officer. 'Do you have anything to declare?' Not having the guts and personality of Oscar Wilde, I couldn't say, 'Nothing to declare except my brilliance.' Nor could I give the reply that my evangelist friend V.M. often gave to startled officers. 'Yes, I have wonderful news to declare about my Saviour – the Lord Jesus. Would you like to hear it?'

In the early seventies I had to be astute and alert when I faced customs officers in certain South East Asian countries. Being a Chinese was a severe disadvantage because these agents often mistook me for a business man loaded with money. I've been regaled with tales of Chinese travellers who had to pay hefty sums of money in order to clear customs. I well remember an occasion when an Indonesian customs officer was sizing me up and asking in Indonesian whether I had anything to declare and if so 'a parting present' would speed me through immigration and customs formality. Although I understood the language, I deliberately replied in English, putting on an Oxbridge accent. As he questioned me further, I spoke as loud as I could so that the other passengers and officers were looking our way. His face turned red like a lobster and he hurriedly waved me on! Later, when I met up with some Chinese Christian friends who had gone to Jakarta, I learnt that they had been relieved of several hundred dollars.

17

Scenes I wish to forget

Beggars in Addis Ababa

There are places that haunt me. How can I forget the sight of young beggars on the streets of Addis Ababa begging for coins and food? They rushed at me when I opened the doors of my host's car. Some of them were deformed; everyone was hopeful for some coins. My host, a Norwegian missionary, had lived in the city for a number of years and he always kept with him a bundle of coins, from which he would give one each to the beggars who milled around us. Later, as we walked into the Mekane Yesus Centre, he explained that some of the deformed beggars have a very unhappy history. Their parents or guardians would sometimes maim them to make them objects of pity, thus increasing their revenue. I shuddered, finding it difficult to hold back my tears.

Poverty in Calcutta

It was December 1984 when I first set foot in Calcutta, a city bustling with people. The streets were dusty and dirty with cow dung and human excrement. It was hot and humid and the mosquitoes made darting flights with their sharp needles to extract blood from my arms, face and legs.

The street vendors were eager to sell me their wares. I walked briskly towards the railway station through the polluted air. Rain brought some relief to the atmosphere. I had to learn to navigate my way through puddles and excrement. I also had to keep an eye on the rickshaws, bicycles, buses and cars that rarely observe the highway code. Soon I arrived at the railway station in Howrah. It was getting dark and amidst the din of loudspeakers and passengers running to catch their trains, I noticed that this huge railway station was gradually being transformed into a gigantic bedroom for the waifs and the homeless of this metropolis. Here and there I saw a man or a young boy pulling unwashed bedsheets from a gunny sack. They tried to find an unoccupied space and in a matter of minutes they were sprawled on the sacks and sheets, trying to sleep. It's hard to forget the homeless in Calcutta. It's equally hard to dismiss scenes like that of a little girl fighting a stray mongrel over a half-eaten *chapatti* (Indian bread) on a rubbish heap. I stopped to wonder whether this undernourished girl would ever live to be an adult.

Too frightening for words – Uganda

In February 1991 I made a return visit to Uganda. I had read about the rapid spread of Aids. A local paper, *Weekly Topic*, described Aids as 'a virus which behaves like a misery-seeking missile in hot pursuit of the Ugandan people'. Their president, Museveni, on World Aids Day 1990, had projected that because of Aids the population would be twenty million instead of thirty-seven million in the year 2000.

This graphic description of Aids as a destructive missile, together with the frightening statistic, came home to me in two frightening scenes. As my colleague drove me into Kampala City there was a temporary hold-up of traffic. I saw a shop selling crudely made, wooden coffins. But what struck me was the fact that there was an equal number of coffins for adults and children. My colleague, Aggrey, commented that it was boom time for coffin-makers because there were so many people dying either of Aids or because of the high incidence of infant mortality. Later, in conversations with various Ugandans, I discovered that in almost every family there was a close relative who had died or is dying of this dreaded disease.

The second scene was at All Saints Church, Kampala. I had arrived to conduct some workshops on Bible exposition for clergy and lay preachers. We were using the church hall; the church itself was packed with mourners. During the lunch break a member of the pastoral staff team of All Saints told me that they were conducting several funerals a week. It was not uncommon for pastors to have three to four burials a week in each congregation.

Aids not only results in the termination and waste of life, it seriously affects the economy too. In Uganda funeral ceremonies attract hundreds or thousands of relatives and friends. All of them have to be fed and entertained by the bereaved family, who in most cases have very limited resources. When a child dies of Aids, his family may have to spend the equivalent of a whole year's income. Besides, families that have living Aids victims are spending huge chunks of their income on traditional cures, quack remedies and witch doctors.

The grim piles of coffins for young and old and the massive attendances at numerous funerals paint a horrifying picture of Aids.

18

Preaching the Word

Spy thrillers

Evangelical preachers benefit immensely from studying the commentaries of Dr Leon Morris, former Principal of Ridley College, Melbourne. I remember first meeting him in January 1968. He welcomed me cordially to his study. It was a massive room and the walls were lined with shelves housing thousands of books. I even noticed a long wooden ladder which I am sure was used frequently by this eminent Bible scholar to reach his books.

As I sat talking to him I was tantalized by a long row of paperbacks located behind his armchair. I scanned the titles and the names of the authors on the spines of these books. Many were familiar to me; they were spy thrillers and detective stories.

When I questioned Dr Morris as to why he read and kept those books so close to his desk, he answered, 'Well, I enjoy reading them. Moreover, they help me to communicate biblical ideas and theological themes simply and succinctly.'

Colourful words

Educational psychologists tell us that an average audience can remember only 5% of a twenty minute verbal communication. Illustrations may well reinforce points and assist retention. Vivid word pictures can also bolster our preaching.

I once heard my colleague Dr Vinoth Rama-chandra of Sri Lanka addressing a group of student workers in the Philippines. Expounding 2 Corinthians 10, he was challenging his audience not to retreat in the face of hostile ideologies. We are not to cave in before man's arrogant thought-systems.

He went on to show that there are four possible responses which Christians can adopt. First, we can be *chameleons*. In the face of anti-Christian ideo-logy, the church changes colour and gives in to secularism, thus losing its distinctiveness. Like chameleons, we merge with the colour of leaves or the bark on the trunk of trees in the forest.

Second, we are not to be *porcupines*. There are some Christians who curl up only to attack their foes. Marxists and Buddhists do not dare to enter our churches because we have our quills ready and aimed at them. We are not adept at winning people to Christ when we act as porcupines.

Third, we are not to be *ostriches*, burying our heads in the sand and thinking that problems will go away with time. Christians have no right to withdraw into ghettos, singing in-group songs and chanting pious slogans.

Paul was no chameleon, porcupine or ostrich. He chose the fourth response: he was more like a *lion*. He challenged the thinking of his day; his confidence was in the transforming power of the gospel. That alone would captivate the hearts and minds of the people. Chameleon, porcupine, ostrich and lion — you don't easily forget such vivid imagery.

The gospel spreads

I sometimes wonder whether churches in England that advertise my name as guest preacher attract or repel people to or from their services. I doubt if I'll ever find out.

In 1982 I was invited to preach during a missionary weekend at Lansdowne Baptist Church in Bournemouth. Nigel W. had been working in that town for a number of years, but he had never ventured into a church since his high school days in Singapore. When he saw my name on the church notice-board he was rather curious and decided to go to the Sunday morning service. He was surprised when he found himself worshipping with several hundred people. He was struck by the joyful singing of the congregation. I preached on the marks of a missionary church, taking the church in Antioch as my example. In my sermon I included instances of God's stupendous actions in bringing men and women to know and serve him.

After the sermon Nigel introduced himself to me. We discovered that we had both come from the same school. Then he exclaimed, 'Your preaching was magic.' An unusual compliment! As we chatted I realized that he wasn't a committed Christian. When I said goodbye, Nigel turned to me and said, 'I'm sure I heard God speaking to me today.'

I introduced him to the pastoral assistant, Gordon Showell-Rogers, who later joined the IFES staff team. Nigel kept going back to this church and even joined the early morning prayer meetings. Soon his spiritual hunger was met and he committed his life to Christ. His new-found faith was incredibly contagious. Within a matter of a few weeks he led his whole family to Christ, including his parents-in-law. His transformed life was an eloquent testimony at his place of work and some of his work-mates were converted. In the short space of a year, twenty-two folk attributed their conversion to Nigel!

When I returned to Lansdowne Baptist Church in 1986, Nigel had emigrated to New Zealand, but it was inspiring to meet some of his relatives and former colleagues at work who had come to know the Lord Jesus through Nigel's witness. One of them shook my hand and said, 'Thank you for pointing Nigel to Christ. God used him to bring me and my family to new life in Christ.'

There is a tremendous encouragement in the ripple effect of preaching.

Unpredictable but powerful word

There is always an inherent danger when a preacher is also a writer. In 1984 IVP published 'Dear Mum and Dad . . .', a book on how to honour and love our parents. So in 1987, when a church in Liverpool invited me to preach, I was assigned the theme 'Honouring your Parents'. It wasn't a topic that I would have chosen myself. I would have preferred to expound a passage.

I preached, stressing the biblical principles of honouring, obeying and loving our parents. I spoke of the need to allow God's Holy Spirit to fill us with love so that we can respect and relate positively to parents with whom we may find it difficult to get along. Suddenly I sensed a strange nudge or prompting: 'Include step-parents.' I did, and I urged the people present to love their step-father or step-mother. I thought no more of it.

After the service when I was shaking hands with people, a young lady took me aside. She was weeping uncontrollably and then she shared: 'God has spoken directly to me through you. For the past two years I have hated my step-mother. Quite frankly, I was even plotting how I could get rid of her once and for all by poisoning her this week. Then God's word found its target – my rebellious heart. I have asked his forgiveness and now I'm going home; and with his strength I'm going to honour and love my step-mother. Will you please pray for me so that I can do this?'

Not quite word-perfect

In 1978 I was giving a series of expositions on leadership to around sixty students. They were all members of Christian Unions in Nairobi, Kenya. After the Sunday service ended there was a gap of three hours before we were due to have lunch. The students went to their respective churches and a few told me that they were going to preach.

Over lunch I asked these budding preachers how they had got on. Three of them nodded with enthusiasm and proudly declared that their message had been well received. I then enquired, 'What did you preach on?'

They replied almost in unison, 'Your sermon.'

I later learnt that my morning exposition had been repeated six times in six different congregations, but the student preachers had adapted my illustrations and applications for their hearers.

19

A window on prayer

A missing dimension

On two occasions I met with evangelical leaders here in England and also in Australia. They were all placing a high premium on expository preaching. I was, of course, overjoyed with this emphasis in their ministry. However, after speaking at their conferences I sensed that a crucial dimension was missing – prayer.

The preaching was superb – solid exegesis, well-crafted sermons and useful down-to-earth applications. Minds were fed and hearts were warmed, but the hearers were never summoned to pray through the message, either individually or in small groups. Is that the reason why these churches and preaching trusts have not experienced a sovereign visitation of God's Holy Spirit?

In lands where God's Holy Spirit works with mighty power, I normally witness church leaders, as well as the ordinary members, at prayer. The South Korean Christians retreat to prayer mountains to spend time in God's presence. They fast and pray; early morning prayer meetings are woven into the fabric of prayer life. No wonder so many people sense the presence of the Lord when they gather for worship services.

Praying with one voice

It is customary for large groups of Christians in South Korea, China and Africa to voice their praises and petitions to the Lord with one heart and voice. For me, I had to get used to this corporate form of oral petitioning. I must confess that I found this type of prayer unusual and awkward for me because I prefer silent meditation and working through lists of prayer requests. In the prayer meetings which I lead or participate in we usually divide ourselves into small groups and we spend considerable time articulating various concerns to God. I suppose there is order and when we pray we are forced to listen to one another so that we can add our intelligent 'Amen' or audible 'Yes, Lord'.

Some years ago I was in Tanzania and observed some villages petitioning their chief to request the municipal authorities to increase the number of pipes carrying water to their community. Although I couldn't understand Swahili, I was struck by their zealous and enthusiastic petitioning. There was volume and passion. People spoke together and when one of the petitioners gave a good reason for their request, the others nodded and chanted 'Yes' in unison. The village headmen certainly got the message.

I realize that God is a generous and gracious heavenly father, but I feel that he is deeply touched and moved when his children express their concerns and needs collectively with urgency and in the spirit of unity and harmony. So nowadays, whenever I am in parts of Africa and East Asia, and when believers are exhorted to pray with one heart and one voice, I join in with great enthusiasm; and to my surprise I find myself greatly refreshed.

Let prayer flow naturally

I once spoke to Roger Mitchell, a former IFES colleague. He is now a leader in the Ichthus Fellowship, a church in south-east London which has experienced phenomenal growth. When asked the secret of rapid growth, Roger told me that his church members seek to be salt and light in their community. They are always willing to give a helping hand to those in need – the lonely, the aged and the marginalized. Some of the younger members of the church would go shopping and even do the gardening for older people. However, what has the biggest impact on their ministry is that they pray for folk in need. So whenever they go visiting in the neighbourhood, one of the questions they ask is whether there is anyone ill or in any kind of need in the family. Then they pray, very often on the doorstep; often the sick are healed and the people are much more open to visits from the Ichthus Fellowship. Others, because they have encountered God's presence through his people, have opened their hearts and lives to him.

I must confess that when someone comes to me with a deep need, I tend to start with the spiritual: Is he converted? Why is he asking us to pray for healing? Is he primarily concerned with his physical well-being or should we show him the importance of his eternal soul? In recent months I have become convinced that members of our church should just pray for people who are sick, fearful or facing personal crises. I have been astounded at how open non-Christians are when they are being prayed for. I think of a lady who was brought to our church by her cousin. She was suffering from cancer and the elders gathered round to pray for her.

The following week she went to a hospital in London, but the doctors could find no trace of cancer. There was great rejoicing and, out of gratitude to the Lord, she welcomed Jesus into her life. For some weeks she was given special instruction, and on Easter Sunday 1991 she was baptized.

You can pray for wedding guests too

When our son, Andrew, was married on 13 April 1991, he and his wife, Debbie, were keen to share God's love in a natural way with their friends and relatives. I had the privilege of preaching the wedding sermon and was able to incorporate a gospel slant in it. But it was at the reception that the Lord began to touch certain lives. A lady with a painful back and slipped disc was telling an elder from our church about her excruciating pain. He, naturally, asked her whether she would like him to pray for her healing. After dinner they retired to a corner of the reception room and he prayed for her. Next morning the pain had gone; the slipped disc was in place. When she went to see her physiotherapist the following week, she was told that there was no need for her to return because she was 'normal' again. She has never stopping telling her friends what happened and we are praying for a definite conversion.

20

Conferences can make a big difference

I have always been amazed by what is accomplished by conferences which have clear goals and objectives. There is always the danger of people going to a conference for a good time of fellowship or simply for a spiritual boost. The effects don't last very long.

A time for harvesting

In July 1972 I spent two days at a conference for high school students in Taiwan. There were around 600 people, half of whom were Christians and half of whom were not. A number of the Christian graduates took time off from their work to serve as counsellors at these special evangelistic camps. At the end of that particular conference, nearly half of those who were not Christians committed their lives to Jesus Christ. Their Christian friends who were with them were responsible for the follow-up.

When I spoke to the staff, they told me that these

conferences always attracted seeking students. For a start, they would love to go to a picturesque centre to get away from the crushing demands of study and family commitments. Secondly, they were always impressed by the sense of purpose and spirit of joy in the Christians. This prompted them to find out the source of such enthusiastic living. Personal kindness and service also mean a lot to students who grow up in a 'dog eat dog' society.

My mind staggers as I try to work out some of the statistics that were given to me. Each year, between 6–8,000 high school students go to these special evangelistic camps. Half are non-Christians and approximately 50%, in turn, are converted. This means that around 2,000 students become Christians through these summer camps. Multiply that by over thirty years of regular conferences and the number of folk converted through these gatherings is remarkably high.

A Japanese conference

In March 1969 I was one of the speakers at a special evangelistic camp organized by our Japanese movement, KGK. There were about sixty university students and about a quarter of them were non-Christians. At our first meeting we were all asked to introduce ourselves, stating our names, courses of study and why we had come to the conference. I knew that the Japanese were traditionally very reserved and would not declare their intentions openly. Much to my surprise, I was proved wrong. The non-Christian participants openly declared that they had come to find out who Jesus Christ really was and whether there was any meaning to life. Some even shared openly their religious pilgrimage. This meant that the Christians present were able to discuss issues openly with their seeking friends.

At that conference I met a Japanese student reading a Greek New Testament. I spoke to him through an interpreter. My first sentence was easy to surmise, 'You must be a theological student. Where are you studying theology?'

He looked up at me with a rather puzzled demeanour, then shook his head, 'I am not a theological student. I have been learning Greek so that I can read the original records of the life and teaching of Jesus.' I have rarely met a more earnest seeker. One of the Japanese staff members spent some considerable time assuring him that the Japanese Bible was a fairly reliable and accurate translation from the original.

At the same conference I was introduced to the regimented behaviour of Japanese people. We were using a government conference centre. Once a day we had to troop into the gymnasium, where the resident PT master led us through some rigorous exercises. Then in the afternoon we had to stand by our beds, and when the loudspeaker barked a command, we had to strip our beds, fold our sheets nicely and then remake our beds. I suffered greatly from an inferiority complex because neat bedmaking is a discipline which I have never been able to master!

Training students: Filipino style

In East Asia, when students come from pagan or Roman Catholic backgrounds there is a great need to inculcate biblical teaching, habits and lifestyle to students. In 1967 I travelled to Kawayan Campus.

This is about 30km from Bacolod City. We lived in wooden houses with thatched roofs. I was glad that these were built on stilts because amongst the tall grass lurked a number of different species of snake. On my first night, when I forgot to take my torch with me when returning to my hut, my imagination ran riot. I was praying that I would not step on any snake.

It was quite an experience to live and work with Filipino students for three weeks. For me it was a new experience, since the longest conference I had been to before had been about ten days long. During the first week students and staff were on their best behaviour. Someone made the joke that we were a conference of 'angelic' students. But during the second week, because we were rubbing shoulders and treading on one another's corns, there were frictions and tensions. What an opportunity it was for us to demonstrate the need for confession, repentance, acceptance and reconciliation. A few days were spent away from the camp-site. Most of the students were involved in what was called 'commando evangelism'. This was an attempt to share the good news of Jesus with strangers in the neighbouring university campus. Practical field-work is invaluable. Later, when the conferees returned for evaluation, new insights were gained as to how best to share the gospel effectively.

In many ways training conferences are strategic investments. For the student movement in the Philippines, it meant equipping student leaders for dynamic leadership in their campus groups.

Training staff

Staff training conferences foster a strong sense of belonging to a movement. Often workers are ministering in isolated areas. I have repeatedly witnessed renewal taking place as workers open their hearts and share their struggles and joys. I suppose we all suffer from the syndrome which says that we are only ones facing unique sets of problems. When others admit that they are in similar situations, our problems are set in their right perspective.

Training conferences not only provide new skills, they also help us to see how others tackle particular tasks and challenges, and how they surmount obstacles. More important, by being away at a conference, I can have a more objective view of my work and achievements. This helps realistic planning.

I have attended many international Christian gatherings and consultations. Novice participants look to the plenary sessions for inspiration and direction, but the more mature participants will inevitably testify that they gain most from their interest groups.

During the Lausanne Congress on World Evangelization in 1974 I talked to a wide range of delegates from different continents. Those who benefited from this unique ten-day gathering were rapturous about their new partnership commitments. For example, leaders involved in Christian literature and TV/radio communications sought out people who were involved in their area of ministry. As a result, bold plans for co-operation were established. Young and radical theologians met to draw up a more radical statement to supplement the historic Lausanne Covenant. Mission leaders from Asia, Africa and Latin America were exchanging information and sharing plans on how they could co-operate and serve side by side in fulfilling the missionary mandate. Had these people simply stuck to the regimented programme they would have gained something, but not as much as they were able to gain by meeting with like-minded participants.

21

Leadership concerns

Lessons from tour guides

We once went on a conducted tour to picturesque Kweilin, China. There were twenty people in our tour party. For five days we went on boat trips, climbed hills, trekked into brightly-lit caves, meandered through markets and ate at different restaurants and hotels.

We were a mixed group and that meant that our walking pace varied. Most were individualistic in their shopping habits and would not show up at the agreed location at the appointed time. The China Travel Service wisely assigned two tour guides to each group of twenty tourists.

The chief guide set the pace and we followed her. Her assistant was mainly responsible for rounding up those who lagged behind or who had become side-tracked. He was remarkably patient; he simply smiled as he rounded up the stragglers.

I thought it would be a great idea if in all our small Christian groups we appointed two leaders. The task of the main leader is to lead the group forward, whilst the co-leader or assistant is around to encourage those who struggle in their faith and those with more reserved temperaments. They need gentle shepherding. The leader who is eager to guide the group forward is easily frustrated if he has to backtrack and round up the 'weaker' members.

Spiritual leadership for all?

McLean Presbyterian Church, Virginia, is a thriving church and the spiritual home of several senators, congressmen and key decision-makers in the USA. In 1989 I was invited to speak at its missions weekend and also conducted a workshop on spiritual leadership. That workshop attracted a number who were presidents and middle managers of large business corporations; a few held responsible posts in different government agencies, including the FBI. I was taken aback when one of the latter asked me whether IFES had a job for him. He knew Russian and was keen to use his linguistic fluency and work experience for God's kingdom.

I sketched the biblical portraits of leaders as servants, stewards and examples, and stressed service and responsibility. Nearly all the participants endorsed what I had to say about spiritual leadership. But the pressing question was whether the principles, ethos and concepts spelt out so clearly in the Scriptures are applicable in the secular world. The president of a multinational company said that most of his colleagues would prefer to adopt the leadership style of Lee Iacoca. They admired his tough, confrontational style of leadership. He was successful in turning the ailing

Chrysler company from a loss-making to a high profit-making motor outfit. (It must be noted that this was just a temporary turnaround, because in 1990 company results indicate a downturn in its fortunes.)

A stimulating exchange followed. Some felt that the biblical principles only apply to leadership in Christian churches and organizations, or at best are simply idealistic. Others disagreed and, from their own experience, cited cases where the biblical principles of care and even servanthood had solved potential employer-employee tensions.

I referred to Tom Peters and Nancy Austen's influential book *A Passion for Excellence,*[1] where they commended leaders who were as tough as nails and uncompromising in their value systems, but who cared deeply about people. Their famous leadership formula was MBWA, which stands for 'Managing By Wandering Around'. They maintain that the manager of a huge department store can only do a good job if he or she walks around encouraging the shop assistants and talking to customers to find out what they are pleased with and what complaints they have about the store. They dubbed MBWA as 'a technology of the obvious'. The simple biblical imagery is that of the shepherd getting around, knowing his sheep and caring for them. I also cited Max DePree's excellent book *Leadership is an Art*[2] where he advocates covenant leadership. He wrote that:

> A covenant relationship rests on a shared commitment to ideas, to issues, to values, to goals, and to management processes. Words such as love, warmth and personal chemistry are certainly permanent. Covenant relationships are open to influence.

They fill deep needs and enable work to have meaning and to be fulfilling. Covenant relationships reflect unity, grace and poise. They are an expression of the sacred nature of relationships (pp. 55–56).

But after the workshop was over, I reflected, 'Time is at a premium for most people, including Christians. If I run spiritual leadership seminars, should I not integrate the principles of biblical leadership so that they become relevant and practical even in "secular" fields, such as the market place and political arena?'

The leaders we choose

I enjoy reading and analysing the components and secrets of successful businesses, sports teams, churches and Christian organizations. What are the key factors and the dynamics involved in high achievement levels and outstanding performances? In almost every case you can trace this to the president, managing director, coach, captain, pastor or chief executive officer who transmits clear vision, sets and maintains priorities and who has the ability to recruit and motivate their leadership teams.

Winners have the flair of attracting winners; they are not surrounded by clones and 'yes-men'. One wit has described 'yes-men' as those who stoop to concur! Only insecure leaders need these hangers-on to boost their egos.

David Ogilvy, the distinguished advertising executive, would send newly-promoted office managers in his company a Russian doll from Gorky. As each smaller doll is unpacked, the manager will find in the smallest doll a message: 'If each of us hires people who are smaller than we are, we shall become a company of dwarfs. But if each of us hires people who are bigger than we are, we shall become a company of giants.'

Three snapshots of evangelical statesmen

My job as General Secretary of IFES often meant meeting important evangelical leaders. Sometimes this meant sharing the same preaching platform, and on other occasions working together on international committees. Here are a few close-up snapshots of three evangelical leaders who have made and are still making a tremendous impact in the world and on the church.

Dr Donald McGavran

Just before my election as General Secretary of IFES, I thought it was both in the interests of IFES and of myself that I should take six months off for reflection and special studies. I chose to spend those six months at the School of World Mission, which is part of Fuller Theological Seminary in Pasadena, California.

Missions in the early seventies were beginning to feel the impact of the church growth movement. I recall my predecessor, C. Stacey Woods, saying to me, 'I hate to admit this, but the church growth school is probably the most significant movement today. I have some reservations about its theology and I even question its methodology. But we cannot ignore its contribution to the world-wide church. Now that Dr Art Glasser is succeeding Donald McGavran as the new dean, it may not be a bad idea for you to spend six months studying under him.'

With the promise of a partial scholarship and IFES support, I enrolled for an MA degree in Missiology. So in late September 1971 I arrived at this famous school.

At first I was disappointed that Dr McGavran wasn't taking our class on the principles of church growth. However, although Dr Glasser was giving us these lectures, I soon discovered that we could not escape the thinking and influence of Dr McGavran himself, who had left stacks of notes and questions for us to work through. At each class session we had to work through twelve to fifteen questions and these were based on his book *Understanding Church Growth*.[1] To answer the questions we had to read every line of this monumental volume. This meant that there was hardly time for us to raise questions and to challenge certain of his assumptions. Later I learnt that Dr McGavran was keen for us to grasp his principles thoroughly so that we could use them as tools to evaluate growth or stagnation of churches around the world.

Dr McGavran gave lectures on a case study of the growth of the Methodist Church in Ghana (formerly the Gold Coast). It was fascinating to listen to him. Although he was in his mid-seventies, he spoke with tremendous conviction and enthusiasm. He gave us detailed outlines and made us read Arthur Southen's book *Gold Coast Methodism*. His thesis was simple: here was a church which was planted in the 1830s and grew into a formidable cluster of churches. Why did it grow? A neat theological answer would be because of the sovereignty of God and the receptivity of the people. But Dr McGavran did not leave it there; he made us discover the political, social, anthropological and religious reasons for the wildfire spread of the Methodist Church in the Gold Coast.

Dr McGavran's approach was unique. He did not simply study the growth of this particular denomination but contrasted it with churches of other denominations within the Gold Coast and the neighbouring nations. For example, I still remember him showing us statistics of the slow growth of the Lutheran Church in Liberia, a country which was only 600 miles away from Ghana. After ninety years of missionary labour this church could only boast 2,000 members, whereas the Methodist Church in the Gold Coast could claim over 200,000 members in the space of fifty years.

As we studied the social, economic and political background of the Gold Coast we discovered that the most responsive group of people were the Fantis. These were Ghanaians who lived on the coast. In the 1830s the British had begun to colonize and administer the Gold Coast. They protected Fantis from being decimated by their traditional enemies, the powerful Ashantis. Partly because of the great prestige of the English, and the arrival of English Methodist missionaries, the Fantis turned in droves to the church and were instructed and baptized. Soon there was the introduction of cocoa and as a result new roads were built and there was a hunger for English education. Mission schools were thus constructed. In reading Southen's book you could never forget the unusual ministry of Thomas Birch

Freeman. He was a man of mixed descent and one of his parents was originally a slave in the Caribbean. Because of his strong constitution and blood group, he did not fall a victim to the dreaded malaria. Thirteen of the twenty-six missionaries who served in the Gold Coast died from this terrible disease within six months of arrival. Dr McGavran forced us to look hard at factors which contribute to or hinder growth.

As I listened to him and got to know him on a more personal level, I began to appreciate his passionate concern to spread the gospel to the unreached. He advocated research and the mobilization of people of high spiritual calibre to fulfil the missionary mandate. The goal was always to plant churches and to work towards growth.

He was always proud of his students and solicitous for their welfare. When he knew that my family were away from me, he and Mrs McGavran invited me to their home. When I successfully defended my MA dissertation, he was the first to put his arm around me to congratulate me. In 1974 I gave him a copy of a paper I wrote for the Lausanne Congress, 'Evangelization of Whole Families'.[2] He spent part of the evening reading through my paper, and the next day there was a short note in my pigeon hole: 'A great paper! I would have given you an A+.' The following year I was in India and was deeply troubled by nominal Christianity in Christian states like Assam and Nagaland. These were states which had experienced remarkable people movements when whole towns, villages and communities turned to follow Christ. I wrote to Dr McGavran to question the danger of numerical growth without stressing repentance and Christian ethics. While the Christians in northeast India did profess faith in Christ, I compared them rather unfavourably with our Indian evangelical student movement, whose members served to exemplify the gospel by their lives and witness. He wrote back a gracious letter admonishing me over my comparison, and recommending that some of our Indian Christian graduates should be more patient with their less literate brothers and sisters in the faith, and seek by example and instruction to reform and renew the church.

The lasting legacy that I have received from Dr McGavran, for which I am profoundly grateful, is a mind which probes and asks questions about why a particular Christian movement is growing or not growing, while at the same time trying to discern patterns in society and culture that would facilitate the advance of the gospel.

Dr Billy Graham

Billy Graham was already a household name before I first met him. I had already read his books and sermons and heard him preach through films and telecasts.

In December 1972 we were together as members of the Planning Committee for the Lausanne Congress on World Evangelization. There were about thirty of us – twenty-five members of the committee and the rest were staff members. That morning I was asked to lead the devotions and gave a brief exposition on Ephesians 6:18–20. I spoke on the four 'alls' of prayer and applied these to the pressing need to intercede for the forthcoming congress. After that period of devotion, we had to move to the floor above us where we had our special meeting room. I entered the lift and found myself standing next to Billy Graham. I introduced myself and, to my surprise, he said, 'I have heard of you. You are the new General Secretary of IFES and I know your predecessor, Stacey, fairly well. I liked your sermon and have made notes on it. I am going to use your four points and preach from them the next time I'm asked to speak on prayer.' Wow! That was a generous compliment to pay a young preacher like myself.

Over the years I have been on other committees or speaking teams with Billy Graham. In spite of his reputation and high profile I have always found him to be a humble and gracious person. He does not dominate team discussions. I observe that he always takes a personal interest in team members and contributes just like other members. So the close-up shots of this man of God match those of that dynamic preacher whom millions see in stadiums, huge arenas and on the TV screen.

Dr John Stott

John Stott has been an example and mentor to many Christian leaders. I count it a rare privilege to be included in that circle.

It was on Easter Sunday 1957 that I first encountered him. He was preaching on the Laodicean church, the last in a series of seven expositions of the churches in Revelation. I had only just arrived in England; in fact it was my first Sunday. I was completely bowled over by the clarity and power of his sermon. I remember writing home to my local pastor, giving a rave review of John as a preacher and of the way in which God used the message to rebuke my complacency and lukewarm attitude.

I have never ceased to marvel at the clarity,

simplicity and power of John's preaching. Each sermon bore the imprint of thorough preparation and disciplined craftsmanship. When I became a theological student he was my model preacher. On one occasion I almost reproduced his whole sermon when I had to preach at an Anglican church in Manchester.

On two occasions I invited him to conduct expository preaching workshops at IFES conferences. He was always at pains to challenge his fellow-preachers and those who were learning to herald God's word to allow the text or passage to determine the message. He stressed the unique role of the preacher as a bridge-builder, relating the world of the Bible to the contemporary world. I have always sat spellbound listening to the introductions of his expository sermons. Within a few minutes he would present a contemporary issue and then introduce his Bible passage, showing how incredibly relevant God's word is to that issue. Like many others, I have been challenged to dig deep into God's word and to ensure that my exegesis is accurate. At the same time, I have to be disciplined in my reading so that I can detect the trends and influences which are shaping the mindset of men and women today.

I shall never forget the day when John shared with some of us that he would always prepare his sermons on his knees. It is in this posture of humility and reliance on the Holy Spirit that he listens to God speaking through his Word.

I owe John a tremendous debt because it is primarily through him that I sought to major on expository preaching, and this has enriched my life and ministry considerably.

It was in August 1963 that I got to know John as an apologist and evangelist. I was then staffworker for FES-Singapore and Malaysia and he was conducting missions at both the University of Malaya and Singapore. I served as his assistant. Through his lectures he answered the questions of seekers and doubters. His words were well-chosen and his arguments convincing. As an apologist, he was able to weed away the doubts and to clear away obstacles to meaningful faith. As an evangelist he effectively pointed his hearers to Jesus Christ as man's only Saviour and Lord. At the same time he preached on repentance and urged his hearers to count the cost carefully. At times he appeared to pour cold water on those who would respond to Christ, in that he was like our Lord and Master, who did not mince his words regarding the cost of discipleship (see Luke 14:25ff.).

On one occasion, when he invited those who had prayed a prayer inviting Jesus into their lives to come and speak to him so that he could give them a booklet and introduce them to a counsellor, there was no movement or response from the crowd. I was standing next to him and, with a heavy heart, he lamented over the unbelief of his hearers. He longed passionately for folk to repent of their sin and to receive the free offer of salvation in Christ.

As an author, it was in 1957 when John's well-known book, *Basic Christianity*,[3] first made its appearance. King Ling was then a second-year chemistry student at Bedford College, University of London. She had been seeking, and some of her CU friends had been witnessing to her. She bought a copy of *Basic Christianity* and read it from cover to cover. When she had finished reading the last chapter, she invited the Lord Jesus into her life. Over the years we have never ceased to recommend and give this helpful book to seekers.

John has written over thirty books, and his

expository messages are preserved in the excellent IVP series *The Bible Speaks Today*, of which he is the New Testament editor. I have consulted these volumes and other writings and they have helped me develop a stronger Christian world-view, as well as providing helpful points and materials in a number of my talks and sermons.

As a visionary, John's leadership and vision have made a great impact on God's church throughout the world. As an Anglican church leader he has courageously rallied evangelicals to remain firm in maintaining their biblical faith and testimony, and the building of God's church has been something close to his heart. He spent numerous hours working through the Lausanne Covenant in 1974 and this document in many ways reflected the growing maturity and balance of evangelicals.

John invited me to serve on three committees. The first was the London Lectures for Contemporary Christianity, and the second was to join him and others in forming the London Institute for Contemporary Christian Studies. In both enterprises, his chief concern was to summon Christians to think biblically, especially in the area of social ethics. He was also keen that Christians should penetrate the different strata of society; his deep longing was to see Christians creatively and effectively involved in the arena of politics, industry, trade unions, the media, medical ethics and the like. For three years he served full-time as Director of the London Institute.

The third committee which he invited me to serve on was the Scholarship Committee for the Langham Trust. Each year this trust makes scholarship funds available to key leaders from Third World churches so that they can work for their doctorates in theology. When they have completed their courses, they return to lecture at theological colleges where they train the current and future generations of church pastors and leaders.

As a friend, John has graciously given me time from his busy schedule for personal chats. He has always taken a deep interest in the IFES and in my own ministry. I was pleasantly surprised one day when he was mentioning various prayer requests which we had listed in the IFES 'Praise & Prayer' bulletin. I discovered that he was using this regularly and that he was able to remember names of people who were being prayed for better than I did! He was always solicitous of the welfare of our family, and when our boys went to university he would even write to them inviting them to join some of the special courses for college students organized by the London Institute. 'Uncle John wrote to me,' each of them would tell King Ling and myself, on receiving their letters.

In the early seventies John was a little disappointed that he could not convert me to be an ardent bird-watcher. He was very successful with a number of my IFES colleagues, who are now avid ornithologists. But I am glad that my 'conversion' to John's favourite pastime did take place, albeit in the late eighties. I have learnt the joy and advantage of scheduling an extra day or half a day bird-watching. This also provides me with an unhurried opportunity to get to know my local host.

23

Hyper-spirituality

The Lord forgot to wake me

I had had a long day in Port Moresby, capital city of Papua New Guinea, meeting and speaking to students. So I was glad to be driven to the home of my host late in the night. The student chairman and secretary reminded me that I had to wake up by 4 a.m. the following morning so that I could catch the 6.30 plane for Lae in the Highlands. By 4 a.m. I was up, sitting on the veranda and waiting for these friends to collect me and drive me to the airport.

I became increasingly restless as I looked at my watch. 5.30 a.m. and still there was no trace of the jeep. My host couldn't help me because the student leaders had my air ticket. Besides, he didn't have the foggiest idea as to where the two students were staying.

Finally, at 6.45 a.m., both students showed up in their jeep. 'Praise the Lord!' shouted one of the students. I was fuming, and becoming angrier by the moment. There was no word of apology. Then,

in a nonchalant way, this student explained, 'Last
night before we went to bed we asked the Lord to
wake us up at 3.30 a.m. He must have forgotten.
But don't worry, I believe that the Lord is holding
the plane for you.'

When we arrived at the airport my flight had left
on schedule. I had to wait for another eight hours
before catching the next plane to Lae. So all my
plans for my twenty-four hour visit had to be can-
celled and rescheduled. You can be sure that I had
to do a lot of speaking the truth in love to these two
brothers!

Hyper-spirituality or plain pride?

Some years ago an Asian faith mission enlisted my
help in contacting an evangelical trust for special
funds. They wanted to build additional dormito-
ries to house and train new workers. I was glad to
assist them because the mission had been sending
vast troops of missionaries to different parts of the
continent.

As it turned out, the trustees of that foundation
were also very sympathetic to the vision and work
of that faith mission. They gave me a very simple
questionnaire which the director had to fill in. He
had to submit simple plans and also the budget for
the building programme, and the amount of the
grant required. I told him that I was happy to
endorse his application.

A few weeks later the director contacted me
again and asked whether I could go back to the
trust to solicit funds on his behalf. I knew the rules
that the trustees had set up; they require the
applicant to fill in the questionnaire. That had
apparently sparked off a crisis amongst board

151

members in the mission. Some argued that this betrayed their faith principle. They stressed that if the Lord wanted to provide them with funds through this particular trust, the trustees would send them a cheque.

This faith mission is still using its over-crammed and inadequate facilities. They could have had new buildings if they had filled in the form. I wonder how God felt. Would he endorse their decision, or did he think that the board members were so taken up with their 'sacred cow' – the faith principle – that their pride and obstinacy had caused them to overlook the fact that any reliable trust requires accountability? Even if the trust accepted the application from me on their behalf, by approaching me had they not breached their own principle?

Open sesame! Spiritual passwords essential

A distinguished English Christian leader was speaking to a group of Christian graduates in East Africa. His topic was 'The Christian Faith and Science', and both his content and the presentation were excellent. The first question which he received from the floor afterwards was, 'Doctor, are you saved?'

My friend was startled and then realized that he had forgotten the briefing that he had received from me and from other African Christians. You cannot speak on any Christian topic unless you have first given a brief testimony. At any evangelical gathering, no matter what your topic is, you begin by telling how the Lord saved you, and you greet the audience with, 'Praise the Lord'.

The absence of such revered phrases and 'spiritual' introduction would give the impression that the speaker is either unsaved or an extreme liberal in his theology!

24

Spirit of enterprise

Business and faith

It was in August 1957 when I said a decisive 'No' to
the business world. I was prepared to burn my
bridges built on the hopes of wealth. For ten years
I was single-hearted in pursuing my theological
studies and training, and in church and student
work. I had Christian business friends, but I would
not have dreamt of asking them to advise me about
Christian work. What has Madison Avenue or Wall
Street in common with God's kingdom? For me,
there was a wide gap and even an incompatibility
between the business world and that of the Christian enterprise.

When I assumed responsibility for co-ordinating
student work in East Asia, I realized that some of
our movements were finding it extremely difficult
to cope with growth pangs. You could award top
marks for the dedication and sacrifice of staff. You
could not fault their vision and objectives, which
were sound and God-honouring. But I sensed
breakdowns in communication and time wasted

because of duplication of duties. Some staff even had to spend an inordinate amount of time licking envelopes and sticking on stamps. Frustration reigned.

Consulting can be profitable!

I was thankful that I had the sense and the guts to seek the advice of two Christian graduates in Hong Kong. One was an accountant with a leading multi-national company, and the other ran his family textile business. Our first dinner meeting was revealing. I shared my problems with them. They listened patiently. Then, in a very gentle and helpful way they suggested certain courses of action. We began with the IFES regional office in Hong Kong. They began to ask me how I planned my itinerary, dealt with my correspondence and which tasks were delegated to my secretary and other staff. They were impressed by the growing ministry but were concerned about the way in which I set my priorities.

They also asked detailed questions about the equipment we used. I thought we were pretty advanced because we were using an electric Olympia typewriter. Both men suggested that we switch to an IBM Golf-ball machine (that was *the* typewriter in 1967/8). I was slightly embarrassed and admitted that we were not in a position to purchase such an expensive machine. One of them winked and said, 'Don't worry, we'll see what the Lord will do about that!' Two weeks later I received a telephone call from the IBM office in Hong Kong; a new machine was being delivered to our office and they wanted to make sure that some-one would be there to receive it. Just as I was thinking about how I could possibly cut down other items on the budget to buy this machine, the manager calmly intimated that it had already been paid for.

That event opened my eyes to see the value of a growing partnership between Christian businessmen and our student ministry. They can provide resources when they are convinced that our ministry is worth supporting; they can also give invaluable advice and insights into how to run the work more effectively.

Raising fresh capital

When the IFES East Asian office was relocated to Singapore, I was keen to launch a literature ministry. Our movements were already producing Bible study guides, but these were hastily and simply produced. They matched the needs of our students and were inexpensive. The late sixties were years that made us more aware of the potential of evangelistic Bible studies. Ada Lum, who was then working with me in East Asia, was instrumental in teaching and training scores of student leaders to lead these Bible studies, where non-Christian students can openly study passages from the gospels and, through study and group discussion, discover who Jesus really is.

Our target was to produce attractive Bible study guides at a reasonable price so that our student groups and local churches would benefit from using them. At the same time I was eager to introduce Bible exposition to Christians in Asia and the audio-cassette tape was an ideal medium of transmission (next to live expositors!). But there was a problem of capital.

I returned to Hong Kong and invited six graduates to join me in establishing The Way Press. We all had to buy shares in the new company. When additional capital was required we had to attempt innovative ways of generating income. 1970 was a year when posters, mini-posters and stickers were extremely popular amongst young people. I was introduced to a very gifted graphic artist. Each Saturday we would discuss ideas and designs for posters and mini-posters. The latter, because they had adhesive backs, could be stuck on to boards, walls, bags, cars and books. We used the silk-screen process for producing these. We began by launching two designs and ordered 100 copies each of the large posters, and about 250 copies each of the mini-posters. We invited Christian students to serve as agents and distributors and they were given 20% commission for their sales. To our delight and astonishment, this initial print-run of 200 posters and 500 mini-posters sold out in less than a month. We immediately reprinted them and added new designs. Soon we were marketing them to department stores. They were rapidly snapped up by eager customers, many of whom were not Christians.

The Operation Mobilisation ship *Logos* bought large stocks of these posters and we were thrilled to receive reports that Arabs in the Middle East were buying them.

In Malaysia, a Christian student was approached by a group of Muslim students at his university. They wanted to buy large stocks of our posters. They also asked where the phrases like 'Love never gives up' and 'Love is kind' came from. When they heard these were quotes from the Bible they were curious and asked whether they could either purchase or borrow Bibles. So what was initially conceived as a money-spinner turned out to be an evangelistic tool. It also showed how young people loved colourful designs and words which are wholesome.

As a result of this enterprise we were able to publish dozens of Bible study guides. Ada Lum launched her career as an author with books such as *Jesus, A Disciple-maker* and *Jesus, A Radical* and *Effective Evangelism*. Our newly-acquired capital also enabled my wife and I and a very gifted couple, Kwong Tek and Goldi Chong, to write a book on love, courtship, marriage and family life. We entitled it *Lovers for Life* and it made its début in August 1971. As it was probably the first book written by local Christians, its sales rocketed and a reprint had to be ordered four months after its release. Since then Scripture Union in Singapore have published a revised edition with a reprint.

When we had enough capital for our publishing programmes, we scaled down our poster-production. We preferred our books to generate income. But there again we were not content simply to sell to Christian bookstores; we appointed and mobilized student agents to sell our Bible study guides and books to their churches and their friends. This operation had to be scaled down when I was elected General Secretary of IFES in August 1971.

Selling paintings

Before I assumed my new responsibilities, it was agreed that I should spend six months at Fuller Theological Seminary, working towards an MA degree in missiology. IFES undertook to pay my salary. I was given a partial scholarship which covered most of my tuition fees. But there were only enough funds to enable me to travel alone to the States.

I was glad to have two months all by myself to begin this intensive course, but I would have liked my family to be with me. I did not feel it right to appeal to friends for funds. I spread my concerns before the Lord and I seemed to get the repeated message, 'Trust me and use your entrepreneurial skills.' On my travels in East Asia I had discovered Indonesia as the source of inexpensive oil paintings. I would buy twenty to thirty canvases and these were sold to hotels in Singapore at 250% profit. Just before I left for America we found we had enough money to buy a ticket for my wife and one son. That was an impressive start.

In my second week at Fuller, I saw a notice publicizing an art fair which was to take place in a square close to my seminary. I made enquiries and learnt that I could rent a space for $15 an afternoon. I borrowed a beret and tried to look as 'artistic' as possible. I took several paintings for display and sale. From the profits that day I was able to pay for a child's return ticket.

Through other connections more paintings were sold. As I was preaching most weekends and IFES had agreed that I should keep all the honoraria for my expenses, I soon had enough funds for my family's air tickets. The timing was ideal. Our two older children had just ended their school year. In late November King Ling and our three sons were able to join me at Fuller.

By then I exulted in my success as a salesman, but still had about six unsold paintings. I went to two art fairs hoping to dispose of them. But no matter how hard I tried, not a single painting was sold. It was evident that God was saying to me, 'I have provided enough for you. Be thankful and content.'

Before we left the USA we gave all six paintings away. For five or six years there was no need for me to utilize my entrepreneurial gift. There was hardly time since I was devoting most of my energies to travelling, speaking, training staff, co-ordinating and administering the affairs of IFES from our London based office. In 1977, when our boys were learning to play the piano, cello and violin, we had to invest in a baby grand, and a fairly expensive cello and violin. Andrew and Daniel were becoming rather accomplished musicians and were taking part in competitions and music festivals. They couldn't continue playing on borrowed instruments. The IFES stipend was adequate for our family needs but it would not be sufficient to purchase these relatively expensive instruments.

Making your hobby pay

It was then that I recalled a church warden in London telling me how he made his hobby pay. He was a medical consultant but spent a fair bit of his spare time collecting antique glass bottles. He told me that he used to go searching for these in rubbish dumps and on the banks of the River Thames. In order to acquire more historic bottles he had to sell some of his lesser finds. That ignited a spark in my business brain. At that time I was dabbling in old documents, prints and postcards of Singapore and South East Asia. These were historical materials, so I began to devote some of my Saturday mornings to hunting these treasures. When we were home on furlough in Singapore I was able to sell eighteenth-century maps of South East Asia (then known as the East Indies), old postcards and postal stationery to the national museum and archives. I was even asked whether I would like to be an honorary curator of the museum so that I could purchase historic documents on behalf of that institution. I felt honoured but politely declined. Proceeds from various sales of these documents and a generous gift from my mother-in-law meant that we could buy the baby grand, the cello and the violin.

I know of Christian friends who have seen the hand of the Lord at work in meeting their financial needs. In my case, I believe I was challenged first to trust the Lord, and then to exercise my entre-preneurial gifts. I'm not for a single moment saying that every Christian should emulate me. I must, however, add that these spasmodic ventures did not interfere or interrupt my ministry. I strongly believe in our Lord's statement on faithful stewardship: 'Every one to whom much is given, of him will much be required . . .' (Luke 12:48b, RSV).

God meets the needs of his children in various ways. Some of my friends inherit wealth, others receive unexpected gifts of musical instruments for their children.

25

Writing

The lost art of letter-writing

I am very thankful that we have an early morning letter delivery. I divide my mail into two piles – bills, invoices and junk mail on one side, and personal letters on the other. As I write, Christmas is fast approaching. This year there have been some special letters which I treasure.

Chris Ellison, a former missionary to China and Singapore, who is now in his eighties, wrote a two-page personal response to our family news-letter. Each paragraph contains priceless responses for each member of our family. Chris belongs to a generation of letter-writers whose words communicate warmth and encouragement. We receive a tremendous lift from his notes.

Then there was another handwritten letter from Sir Norman Anderson thanking God for what he has done in IFES and assuring me of his prayers as I move on to a new sphere of service. How very kind of this distinguished writer and Christian leader to write!

There was a contemporary postcard and a few scribbles from a church member, a relatively young Christian, telling me how much my series of expositions on Romans has strengthened her faith and transformed her relationships with the Lord and her friends. I was delighted that she had written to express appreciation. Little does she know how much that puts fresh heart in me. May this tribe of letter-writers increase!

Yes, I do wonder whether the present generation has forgotten the art of letter-writing. I suppose we could all complain about the high costs of postage these days, how an electronic age beckons us to use the phone and how there is warmth in the human voice. But I confess that I prefer the letter; it means that someone has really given thought to expressing something personal and meaningful. Memories of a three-minute phone call tend to evaporate.

The early pioneers of student work were great letter-writers. People like Howard Guinness, Stacey Woods, Charles Troutman, Ada Lum, Samuel Escobar, Hans Bürki, Douglas Johnson, Oliver Barclay and many others used their skills as letter-writers to motivate students and graduates to serve the Lord Jesus. Often their correspondence was recorded on postcards with just three or four sentences, but they brought colossal inspiration, affirmation and encouragement to many.

Letters never smile

My predecessor, Stacey Woods, used to tell me, 'Letters never smile.'

When we need to be firm or to rebuke someone by letter, relationships can easily sour as a result.

How do we overcome the severity of cold print?

I confess that sometimes my letters have hurt their recipients, ones where I had written either in anger or frustration. Often the reasons are justified but the words chosen were too caustic or negative. Does that mean that we should not write these letters? Not at all; that would be irresponsible. Over the years I have learnt that there are four things that I need to do before writing painful letters. First, I need to pray so that my spirit is right with God, and I also pray for the person who will be receiving my letter. Second, I draft a letter and then seek to correct any offensive word or phrase. I also check whether I have balanced my criticism with affirmation of the good things that the person has achieved. Third, I show a corrected version of my letter to a senior colleague. If I were writing to a lady then I would make sure that a senior lady colleague would read it first. However, if I do not feel at peace with the final text, the fourth step is to write a personal note requesting a face-to-face meeting at the earliest possible time. This procedure has saved needless aggravation and has strengthened relationships and communication.

26

Comebacks

Knocked down but not out

I have enormous admiration for politicians,
sportsmen, Christian leaders and missionaries who
stage successful comebacks. The media, with their
army of critics, delight to fire verbal missiles at
those who occupy the centre-stage. They expect
these men and women to stay at the pinnacle of
their profession or sport. Lapses are unmercifully
scrutinized and failures grossly exposed. When a
politician is defeated in an election, or when a top
athlete fails to win the gold medal, he is written off.
Most have no stomach to fight back. Like balloons,
they became grossly inflated when the media-men
puffed them up. They suddenly become terribly
deflated when they find themselves painfully
pricked and slashed by the cutting remarks of the
same band of critics. But there are some who have
the resilience and determination to fight back and
to rise above their critics, who have either prema-
turely written their obituaries, or who have rele-
gated them to the ranks of the also-rans.

165

In the late seventies and early eighties, Sebastian Coe was the greatest middle-distance runner in the world. He won the Blue Riband 1500 metres Olympic event in Moscow. Those who saw him on television will not forget his joy and exultation. From 1982 onwards Coe was dogged by illness and defeats. His athletic prowess and reputation were in tatters. There was no shortage of sports critics advising him to withdraw from the Los Angeles Olympics in 1984. Few thought he would win the 1500 metres but to everyone's astonishment he did win it again. Coe was ecstatic, but in a detailed biography of his magnificent fightback, *Sebastian Coe: Coming Back* by David Miller,[1] we read of Coe turning to the mass ranks of press and television reporters at Los Angeles only to yell, 'Who says I'm finished?' His biographer adds, 'It was triumph over criticism as much as triumph over adversity.' Coe had staged a remarkable comeback and the sports world had to salute him.

I am glad that the Bible is such an honest book. Spiritual giants like Abraham, Moses, Elijah, David and Peter experienced failure and defeat. It was tempting to throw in the towel, but by God's grace they were restored and rose up to complete their assignments.

Restoring grace

I have a pastor friend who almost blew his vocation as a minister of the gospel. He was a very effective evangelist and a much sought-after speaker. Once, when he was on an extended tour, he fell into sin and for a couple of weeks he was involved in an adulterous relationship. Later this sin was exposed and he had to confess it. He resigned from his pastorate and with tears apologized to his congregation for letting the Lord and them down. He took two years off from active ministry and subjected himself to the discipline of four trusted Christians in his community. My friend spent those two years in study, prayer and developing his relationship with his wife and children. The four men exercised pastoral care and discipline over him and after two years he was restored and is now exercising a ministry which has enriched the lives of hundreds.

I was glad that he never excused his sin. Neither would he allow the devil to relegate him to the sidelines so that he would never be able to use his preaching gifts again. His repentance and restoration made many realize afresh the wonder and power of God's renewing grace.

Judo wisdom

There is a beautiful judo adage, 'Never mind if you are knocked down seven times, as long as you get up eight times!'

Making comebacks possible

Sometimes I am terribly alarmed at the way in which some of us older Christian leaders indulge in adverse, negative criticisms of our younger colleagues. We expect them to be consistent and to perform with aplomb. When they fail, we are very swift to point out their faults; we are quick to write them off or to put them down. It is a miracle how some of these fine men and women do survive, so I pray that God will always give me a kinder spirit, a warmer heart, supporting hands and encouraging lips, so that defeated saints can repeatedly make their comebacks.

Once I was talking to a housewife who had become a Christian in her late forties. She was lamenting the chronicles of her wasted years and envying me because I had been serving the Lord since an early age. I said to her, 'You know, there is something simply fabulous and miraculous in our faith and it is expressed in a biblical promise. God said to Israel and he says to us, "I will repay you for the years the locusts have eaten . . ." (Joel 2:25a).'

168

27

Beyond corruption?

Jakarta, Indonesia: July 1969

I had an urgent telegram to send to Singapore. My host took me to the central post office and I duly filled in my telegram form and handed it to the cashier. He quoted a price and I handed him the exact amount. He counted the rupiahs, smiled and nodded. I thought that was the end of our transaction, but he went on to ask me in Indonesian, which I understood, 'What about something for me?'

Here was corruption staring me straight in the face. What was I to do? My host noticed my discomfort and my hesitation. A brief exchange followed between the cashier and my friend, and in the end the latter handed over some rupiahs (equivalent to around 20 US cents) and steered me away from the counter.

When I was about to open my mouth in protest, he gently remarked, 'Wee Hian, I know what you are thinking ... How can a Christian succumb to bribery? As a Christian businessman I face this almost daily. If I hadn't given him the little extra your telegram would never have reached its intended destination. I regarded my contribution as a service charge rather than a bribe. You must understand that these public servants are so poorly paid that their salaries just cannot sustain them, so they have to use their position to extract the extra from their customers.'

Kampala, Uganda: February 1991

I was complimenting David Zac Niringiye on his vision and drive in raising funds for his movement to build a student centre and three staff houses just outside Kampala City. He agreed that it would be a strategic operational base, but lamented the fact that he could not secure a telephone line, in spite of applying for one eighteen months before. I asked, 'Is there a long waiting-list for phones?'

He replied, 'Perhaps, but if we were willing to hand over several thousand shillings (the equivalent of US$100) I'm almost sure that we would get a line next week. We have been praying that God will somehow overrule and that we will not have to resort to bribing the telephone engineers. As you can see, we face a real predicament; as a Christian organization, bribery is completely out of the question. At the same time we have to see things from the engineers' point of view. They are probably earning between $15 and $20 a month, and can't live on peanuts like that. So many have to supplement their meagre incomes with "generous tips".'

I was silent and for some minutes deliberated on what I would do if I were in David Zac's shoes.

Border checkpoint between Ghana and Togo: July 1988

A convoy of six cars left Abidjan, Ivory Coast, bound for Lomé, Togo, where the francophone student movements were convening for their triennial conference. The twenty-four passengers with their six drivers had already spent almost three days travelling before reaching this frontier. At the checkpoint their passports were checked and their travelling documents were found to be in order, but they were not allowed to proceed until money was handed over to the immigration police. As Christians they refused to do this and so they were asked to park their cars and had to wait indefinitely in the extreme heat of West Africa. They expostulated and argued their right to enter Lomé, Togo, but the officers shook their heads, waved their arms and insisted that they should remain there.

Later, an officer approached the group and asked whether it was really worth sticking to their Christian principles, when only a few dollars would see them speedily into Togo. The Christians refused to give up and suddenly one of their leaders suggested that they should start to pray aloud and to sing hymns of praise to God. After all, that was what Paul and Silas had done when they found themselves unjustly locked up in the prison in Philippi. They sang boisterously, and the passengers who were going through immigration and customs took notice, asking why they were there. Even hardened officers can suffer from red faces; before long they walked up to the singing Christians and waved them on.

28

Reflections

On losing my watch

It was 28 January 1983, in Chaclacayo, Peru. Two hours ago I still had my quartz watch on my left wrist, but now it was gone. At 8 p.m. Samuel Escobar and I were walking away from St. Martin's Plaza. The street was crowded and suddenly someone grabbed my arm. Within seconds my watch was gone. It was the first time in my life that I had been robbed of a personal possession. I was quite stunned but prayed: 'Lord, may that thief who now has my timepiece come to know you one day and enjoy eternity with you.'

When we returned to the conference site, a Chilean staffworker remarked, 'Now you'll be able to talk about the Latin American reality from experience.'

Another commented, 'Yes, and you will also be able to understand and feel our pain.'

Encounter with astral spirits

I had spent the morning of 29 December 1990 in rehearsing a sketch for our special evangelistic meeting on 13 January, As I couldn't find any script on the subject of horoscopes and fortune telling, I had had to write a playlet, involving three performers.

King Ling, Daniel and I were watching an interesting TV programme highlighting twenty-five years of royal performances. There was quite a bit of nostalgia as the audience caught glimpses of familiar TV and film stars. Suddenly I experienced a choking sensation. At first I thought that it was the skin of a grape that had caught in my throat. Although the room was warm, I felt cold and began to shiver violently. I began to hear strange noises. I got even more worried when I asked King Ling whether she could hear anything and she assured me that everything was still. Dark clouds then seemed to descend on me. I was frightened and didn't know what was going on. I was seized with fear, especially the fear of dying and there were inner voices telling me that I would not live through the remaining two days of 1990! I quickly picked up the phone and called one of our church elders, urging him to phone around and ask other leaders to pray for me. Then King Ling and Daniel prayed for God to lift the dark clouds and expel the forces of darkness.

I have never ever had such a frightening experience, but in the midst of it I did sense God's peace, because I knew a lot of people were praying for me. The following day I tried to analyse and reflect on what had happened. It suddenly dawned on me that I had been pressing on a raw nerve of the evil one. For several days I had been reading articles, magazines and books on the subject of predicting the future and working out the intricacies of zodiac signs, personal horoscopes, numerology, *i ching* and popular astrology. I had studied these materials in a rather detached way. I was simply gleaning information and trying to understand why men and women today rely so much on astrology. I sense that fear of the unknown and of the spirit world often leads people to try to get on the good side of 'benign' spirits. Unbeknown to me, I seemed to have stumbled into the lair of spiritual powers. Hence the severe attack. I have learnt a very valuable lesson: I cannot be detached when I study forces and movements that are in direct opposition to Christ and his kingdom. I needed special divine protection. That experience forced me to seek God's grace and help as I continued to prepare my sermon for 13 January. I must expose Satan's wiles and traps, but I can only do this in the strength of the Lord.

29

And so to bed

He gives his beloved sleep

I don't think that I could have survived twenty-five
years of constant travelling if God had not given
me this wonderful gift of sleep. When I am
stretched out on a bed, it only takes a few minutes
before I am sleeping like a log. But for twenty or
more years I found it almost impossible to sleep
when travelling on a plane. Intercontinental flights
can take between seven and twelve hours. I think it
was on my first transatlantic flight from London to
New York that I developed a phobia against sleeping while in a sitting posture. On that occasion I
experienced a slight twist in my neck and ever since
I was afraid to sleep, until I was introduced to the
inflatable air pillow. This forms an excellent support for my neck.

In 1965, at a missions conference, I had to sleep
rough with the student campers in Muar, Malaysia.
About twenty of us, all men, had to sleep on a
raised platform. Under the platform were mosquito coils and the whiff of incense-filled smoke

kept the mosquitoes at bay. But when the coils burnt out the mosquitoes had a heyday (or was it a heynight?!) diving at us and sucking blood from our arms, legs and faces. Sleeping together on what was really one giant bed, a comrade spirit developed amongst us. The students were impressed that the speaker did not have a single room all to himself.

Taiwan: July 1972

When I arrived in the city of Tainan, I was very tired and wanted to get to bed as quickly as possible. The local staffworker only had a double bed. Fortunately (or unfortunately) his wife was away visiting her parents and so we both had to sleep on that same bed. There was no guest room in his apartment. I did ask for permission to sleep on the sofa, but he would not entertain that idea. I did pray that somehow he might volunteer to spend a night on the sofa himself! But he insisted that we shared his room. The bed was quite large and comfortable, and there was very little likelihood of either of us kicking the other. We prayed together and I wished him a good night's rest. To my great chagrin, this staffworker began to pray aloud. While I was trying to sleep he was calling out passionately to the Lord. This must have gone on for a couple of hours. The light above us was burning, and it must have been the early hours of the morning before he stopped praying. Then I was able to sleep.

Outside Saigon, Vietnam: June 1970

The war was in full swing, but the people of Saigon (now Ho Chi Minh City) had grown accustomed to the skirmishes between the American forces and the Vietcong. The student movement organized a camp in the outskirts of the city. In the evening we slept on camp-beds made of wood and canvas. Once I had tucked myself into bed, I noticed that my body was only about three inches above the concrete floor. It was around 11 p.m. when the lights went off. As soon as we tried to sleep our whole building rattled. About 2 km away there was a furious exchange of gun-fire. Helicopters were hovering overhead and I was naturally very frightened, but as I looked around the room I saw that the Vietnamese students were sleeping peacefully. The staffworker saw me sliding nervously out of bed and he stretched out his arm to give me a reassuring pat that everything was all right. He casually remarked, 'We're all used to the sound of battle. You'll get used to it too.' I was quite astonished that after another thirty minutes or so I did get used to the din, and fell peacefully asleep.

Da Lat, Vietnam

After participating in the conference on the outskirts of Saigon, we moved north to Da Lat, where there was another conference. We were billeted in a large Christian conference centre. I was overjoyed when I was given a room to myself, but that joy was short-lived ... When I retired to bed at around 10 p.m. I decided to do a bit of reading. The mosquito net protected me from these unwelcome insects. Suddenly I looked up, and to my horror, I noticed that there was a big hole in the ceiling just above my bed. Peering down at me were several pairs of eyes. These were the geckoes (a type of lizard).

In Singapore and Malaysia I was familiar with the tiny lizards; they were harmless creatures and we were always grateful that they would consume flies and fleas. But in this case the geckoes were enormous; their heads at least ten times the size of their 'cousins' in Singapore and Malaysia. Their average length was around 25 cm. My imagination worked overtime. What other creatures were lurking in the ceiling? That night, sleep forsook me and I was glad when morning dawned. I was also relieved when I realized that I only had to spend one night in that room.

Chicago, Illinois: May 1980

My friends at InterVarsity Press were very kind and put me up in a very comfortable hotel. It provided an ideal atmosphere for getting over my jet lag. Just after midnight I must have tried to free my arm from my bedcover, and in so doing touched a mechanism on the side of the bed. The whole mattress began to move, there was a juddering sound and my bed became a rocking-horse. I jumped out of it and soon the movement ceased. I switched on the lights and discovered that my bed was fitted with a massaging contraption. The last occupant must have left a quarter in the slot and it was temporarily jammed. My arm movement must have assisted its descent, so that it triggered off the massaging mechanism. Moral: Modern hotels have surprises in store!

Hospitality Inn

I have sometimes been asked by my host whether I would prefer to live in a hotel or in the home of Christians. In most cases I would choose the latter. Some of my male colleagues have told me of their unpleasant experiences when staying alone in hotel rooms. They have received suggestive calls from prostitutes; some of these women brazenly knocked at their doors. I think we men, whether single or married, when we stay alone at hotels, can become vulnerable to these temptations. Surprisingly, although I have slept in many hotels and boarding houses, I have only been 'propositioned' once, and that was over the phone in a YMCA, of all places. I was having my quiet time and it was easy for me to put the phone down.

Today, most modern hotels have selected video programmes and soft porn films on offer. My passionate plea is that, where possible, Christians should offer room and hospitality to travellers like myself, who need rest, fellowship and protection.

30

Being a global Christian

'It's all right for you to advocate that all Christians should be global Christians. You've travelled constantly and from what you've said, you certainly adapt extremely well to new friends and cultures. My world is rather different. I spend more time with animals than with human beings. My wife and I had to summon up extra reserves of courage just to cross the channel for a day trip to France.' Mr Lester was a dairy farmer from Yorkshire and he rarely minced his words. He was visiting his daughter in Southampton and heard me speaking at a missionary weekend. Before I could comment he went on, 'Moreover, your job and your organization force you to be a world Christian. What about ordinary believers like myself?'

I asked him whether he watched the news on TV. 'Of course I do – every day. I carry a small transistor radio with me and I tune to the BBC World Service.'

'That's excellent,' I retorted. 'That's where I get most of my material for global praying.' He looked rather surprised. I explained that national and world news always provided me with splendid opportunities for intercession. At that time the famine in Ethiopia and Sudan was grabbing the headlines. The tragic scenes of poverty, death and misery triggered me to pray for the leaders of both nations, as well as the victims of malnutrition and famine. I showed Mr Lester *Operation World* by Patrick Johnstone.[1] I explained, 'This is an excellent resource book for global Christians. It's packed with concise information on every nation. When a news item strikes me, I consult this book to find out more about the country that's making the news.'

We decided to check out Ethiopia and Sudan. Within minutes we gleaned vital information on both countries. We studied the population figures and compared the relative strength of the church in both countries with those of the Muslim communities. We immediately discerned that the Christians in southern Sudan were in the majority, but in the north they were in the minority under the Arabs. We read useful statistics about the size and influence of the Ethiopian Orthodox Church and its hostilities towards Protestants. The prayer requests enabled us to target specific prayers for both nations.

By then Mr Lester was getting rather excited. 'Hey this is thrilling! I can be a world Christian where I am; my papers and TV news broadcasts can serve as prompts for prayer. Thank you for introducing me to *Operation World* – where can I buy a copy?'

Thankfully, he was able to purchase a copy from the church booktable.

Other practical ways of being a global Christian

The best place to sow the seeds of global Christianity is the Christian home. Each family should have a copy of *Operation World* within easy reach as they listen or watch news broadcasts together. In November 1989, amidst cataclysmic changes in Eastern Europe, one family felt burdened to intercede for Romania. Hungry for more detailed information, they subscribed to missionary magazines which gave them in-depth information about the spiritual needs of that land. As they watched on TV the plight of neglected children, they took instant action and gave generously to a mission which sought to meet the needs of these unfortunate youngsters. When they heard that a team from a neighbouring local church was planning to take food and clothes parcels to Romania, this family made further contributions.

I know of another family who have taken a personal interest in a missionary family and a national worker. They pray for these workers daily. The children correspond and send magazines and stamps to the children of both these workers serving in Tanzania. Whenever I meet this family, they tell me of the struggles and progress of these front-line troops. For me, this family is exemplary as prayer warriors. They recognized that their missionaries and national pastor were often targets for satanic attacks and by their prayer and practical involvement, all the family members were actually serving as back-up troops.

I have been impressed by local churches and Christian Unions which adopt missionaries and national workers. In addition to regular prayers for these servants of the Lord Jesus, there will be special missionary spots in their programme, so that the entire congregation or Christian Union can be kept up to date on the workers they support. I shall always remember a church prayer meeting where I saw the faces of many members literally light up as they listened to a tape from their missionary working in North India. He was thanking them for their faithful ongoing prayer support and he reported on the marvellous ways in which God was answering their prayers, for example when a Hindu family burnt their idols and turned to the living God. On the same tape his wife expressed her gratitude for the gifts, books and toys which the church had sent her and her family for Christmas. One Christian Union received a special thank-you card from an Indian pastor for making it possible for him to visit his aged parents, who were living several hundred miles from where he was busily proclaiming the gospel and establishing a new congregation. In both the local church and the Christian Union, the members had entered into meaningful partnership with these co-workers. As a result these Christians became cognizant of the hostile setting in which the missionaries and the pastor were working. They identified with them in their spiritual combat against the forces of darkness and they rejoiced when prayers were gloriously answered.

It must be mind-boggling for Christians to seek to obey Christ's great commission to go and make disciples of all nations (see Matthew 28:19). How can anyone do that? Not all are called to be cross-cultural envoys of the gospel, and in fact a large number will probably remain in their home countries to serve the Lord. But in recent years God has brought large numbers of international students to the doorsteps of many university cities and towns. What an opportunity to fulfil the great commission and to be global Christians! By befriending international students, we have unique opportunities to learn more about their country, culture, customs and religion. Most of these students are often lonely and are more than eager to talk about their families and countries.

By opening our homes and hearts to them we can effectively share God's love with them and quite a number of these students, some from so-called closed countries, have committed their lives to Jesus Christ because of those followers of his who genuinely care for them.

A church could motivate and channel members with cross-cultural gifts and abilities to bring the gospel to the unreached peoples. These are folk who have never heard a clear presentation of the gospel; they include those who live in the Muslim, Hindu and Chinese world. They are not in close proximity to a Christian congregation. Pioneer evangelists and church-planters are urgently needed and we must pray that God will send more of these workers. Others could be encouraged to work alongside national Christian leaders as partners in building up God's church. Today, as more countries are closing their doors to traditional missionary task forces, some of our church members with professional skills could be directed abroad as 'tentmakers', supporting themselves and at the same time representing Christ as his ambassadors. It is remarkable to see how God has used Christian teachers and lecturers from the East and West to teach and work in lands like China. By their presence and testimony they have been instrumental in introducing many Chinese students to Christ.

No group of Christians, whether it be a family, Christian Union or church, is ever impoverished by being world Christians. As they share God's concern in serving the needy and rescuing the lost, they will experience his blessing. In my office I have a large wall-map of the world and I have stuck on it a card which someone sent me a few years ago. On it are the words, 'God so loved the world ... He still loves the world!'

31

Parting shots

Some of my friends were rather surprised when they learnt that I was planning to step down as General Secretary of IFES. They wondered why I wanted to leave a fulfilling international job, where there were visible evidences of God's blessing — especially with the gospel making such dramatic advances in the world of students. Had I considered the cost of leaving such an exciting ministry?

I admit that there were moments when I questioned my decision too. That is where life's signposts and bearings can provide clearer directions:

Signpost one

I had been General Secretary for nineteen years. If I add the five and more years during which I was Associate General Secretary for East Asia, that brings my term of service to almost a quarter-century. That is a long stint; I have had a long and good innings.

Signpost two

It has always been my conviction that a growing organization needs to have new blood and fresh creative leadership. There were four or five leaders in the IFES family who could succeed me and lead the movement forward. These men are either in their late thirties or early forties and IFES, being a movement of students, should have younger leadership. Besides, it would be selfish to hog the job.

Signpost three

Whenever I have spoken on leadership, I have always emphasized the need for any leader to ensure that his organization or department is making steady progress. When a captain has to abandon a sinking ship, folk are not going to think highly of his leadership skills and achievements. If I could compare IFES to a ship, I could truthfully say that, by God's grace, it has weathered storms and tempests, and it is sailing on an even keel with an able crew on board.

Signpost four

For more than twenty-eight years my wife, King Ling, has loyally supported me in my ministry amongst students. In the early years she had to look after the home and children whilst I had to travel extensively. Her spiritual gifts complement mine. For example, I think of myself as the Bible expositor, but she is amazingly gifted in training folk to lead effective Bible study groups. Gift-wise,

I am the visionary and strategist, but she is the tactician who can make dreams a reality and can implement plans. It would be a new challenge to serve together in a local congregation.

Signpost five

In an unplanned development we find ourselves involved in the establishing and building up of an international church in London's West End. Our congregation is committed to growth through evangelism, discipleship and missions – goals which are near and dear to our hearts.

All five signposts served as indicators that it was time to hand over my leadership responsibilities in IFES and to move on to a new assignment as the pastoral leader of a young but growing church.

There is, of course, the inner conviction from the Lord that the time is ripe for new adventures. I realize that I will miss the props and resources of IFES when I move to work in a local church. But I am always reminded that our sufficiency is of God. He will provide and lead us forward.

The well-known American architect and designer, Frank Lloyd Wright, was once asked, 'What is your greatest achievement?'

His reply was swift and concise: 'The next.'

I echo his sentiments, but my confidence is not based on my past achievements, experience or abilities. It rests on that tremendous verse of assurance:

'No eye has seen,
no ear has heard,
no mind has conceived
what God has prepared for those
who love him.'
(1 Corinthians 2:9)

Notes

Chapter 4

1 L. Luzbetak, *The Church and Cultures* (Tachny, Illinois: Divine Word Publications, 1970), p. 126.
2 *Ibid.*, p. 129.

Chapter 21

1 T. Peters and N. Austen, *A Passion for Excellence* (New York: Random House, 1985).
2 M. DePree, *Leadership is an Art* (East Lancing, Michigan: Michigan State University Press, 1987), pp. 55–56.

Chapter 22

1 D. McGavran, *Understanding Church Growth* (Grand Rapids: Eerdmans, 1970).
2 Chua Wee Hian, 'Evangelization of Whole Families', in *Let the Earth Hear his Voice* (World Wide Publications, 1975).
3 J. R. W. Stott, *Basic Christianity* (Leicester: Inter-Varsity Press, 1971).

Chapter 26

1 D. Miller, *Sebastian Coe: Coming Back* (London: Sidgwick and Jackson, 1984).

Chapter 30

1 P. Johnstone, *Operation World* (4th edition: Bromley: OM Books and WEC International, 1986).